Debbi DiGennaro has an easy, con
insights into life in Africa for the Westerner. Her years of living in Africa
have given her perspective in such a way that she clearly explains many
cultural differences in an honoring way. I highly recommend this book
to people who seek to find appropriate ways to relate to their African
colleagues and friends.

Sarah Lanier, *author of* Foreign to Familiar

Debbi DiGennaro's book is an extraordinary book of wisdom for those who
want to serve Africa. I commend it as a proven roadmap to a continent of
adventure and beauty.

Floyd McClung, *founder of All Nations*

I want to make the finished book required reading for all missionaries with
[our organization].

Andrew Steer, *management consultant with African Inland Church*

This book is a must-read for anyone considering living outside their own
culture.

Jon Parsons, *founder of Turning Point Ministry*

Acclimated to Africa
Cultural Competence for Westerners

SIL International®
Publications in Ethnography

45

The Publications in Ethnography series focuses on cultural studies of minority peoples of various parts of the world. While most volumes are authored by members of SIL International® who have done ethnographic research in a minority language, suitable works by others also occasionally form part of the series.

Managing Editor
Eric Kindberg

Volume Editors
Mary Huttar
Dirk Kievit

Copy Editors
Bonnie Brown
Dawn Escoto
Barbara Shannon

Production Staff
Lois Gourley, Composition Supervisor
Barbara Alber, Compositor
Barbara Alber, Cover Design

Cover Photos
Foreground image by Peggy Connett;
Background image by Ikiwaner:
https://commons.wikimedia.org/wiki/File:Kiang_West_savanna.jpg,
"Kiang West savanna", image modification by Barbara Alber,
https://creativecommons.org/licenses/by-sa/3.0/legalcode

Contributing Artist
Debbi Omondi

Acclimated to Africa

Cultural Competence for Westerners

Debbi DiGennaro

Foreword by Laurenti Magesa

SIL International®
Dallas, Texas

© 2017 by SIL International®
Library of Congress Catalog No: 2017953253
ISBN: 978-1-55671-386-6
ISSN: 0-0895-9897

Printed in the United States of America

Copies of this and other publications of SIL International®
may be obtained through distributors such as Amazon,
Barnes & Noble, other worldwide distributors and, for select
volumes, www.sil.org/resources/publications:

SIL International Publications
7500 W. Camp Wisdom Road
Dallas, Texas 75236-5629 USA

General inquiry: publications_intl@sil.org
Pending order inquiry: sales@sil.org

Contents

Foreword

For most of the nearly seven decades of my life I have lived and worked in Africa. But I also have spent almost ten years living and working in the West, namely, in America and Europe. One thing I have noticed in both worlds during this pilgrimage has been the expectation of me by the "natives" or "locals" in each of these locations to be able to speak their "language." This has meant that I have been presumed to acquire, to some degree, the basic skills of their thinking and behavior patterns. Over the years, I have learned not to be surprised or upset by this.

As a Christian minister I have been privileged to serve different communities in my ecclesiastical province in northwestern Tanzania where there are more than twenty-five ethnic communities living in relatively close proximity to one another. In many cases, people from different ethnicities even live together in the same community. Ministering in these various localities of the province, I have experienced obvious approval and easy acceptance whenever I have demonstrated what, in their view, amounted to a satisfactory measure of cross-cultural skills. On the other hand, I have detected open or subtle resentment whenever, again from their perspective, this cultural familiarity has not been sufficiently deep; and my hosts, in such cases, seemed to resign themselves to my "indomitable ignorance." Their outlook amounted to a "we-cannot-expect-him-to-know-better" sort of thing.

It is in the West that I have found the expectation to acquire their social philosophies and skills quite stark and unapologetic. There, people have generally taken exception even to my African-English accent, as well as my lifelong, culturally-conditioned, body language and mannerisms. Of course I have tried to do whatever I could to fit in.

Upon returning to Africa with this experience overseas, I have frequently wondered why quite a few of my missionary colleagues from the West have not changed their relational skills with Africans, despite the fact that some of them have spent ten, twenty, or even thirty years working in close proximity to African peoples. I have asked myself the question: "Why have these friends of mine not acquainted themselves with some of the basic elements of the African language of life?"

Furthermore, it becomes even more perplexing when the Westerner, as a guest in Africa, expects in a not-so-subtle way his/her host in Kajiado or Nyahururu to exhibit social etiquette proper to Birmingham or Los Angeles. Of course, for hospitality's sake (a value almost sacrosanct in Africa), the African will in general outwardly comply with such anticipations. However, it would be a mistake to assume that the African is satisfied with this situation. But the error in social etiquette is commonplace in relationships between Africans and Westerners in Africa. It is one that urgently needs to be corrected in the interests of genuine, intercultural respect and mutuality.

This is where *Acclimated to Africa: Cultural Competence for Westerners* fits in. This book comes as a corrective to the dissonance in intercultural relationships between Western "guests" and their African "hosts." It is actually intended as a guide, as its subtitle indicates, to equip Westerners living in Africa with some basic principles to appreciate their hosts' interpersonal customs and to relate with them accordingly. The book is a training manual of life-etiquette for Westerners in Africa.

In the characters of Juma and Wesley, the author demonstrates a sharp, witty, and sensitive eye to the demands of African and Western intercultural relationships in Africa. With neat, pithy aphorisms, she captures the essential philosophies of both groups toward the basic dimensions of life. The picture that emerges is, indeed, one of deep, cultural contrasts.

The point of the book is that the differences can, in fact, be extremely beneficial for intercultural harmony when handled properly. Acknowledging and appreciating these differences can help the Western guests in Africa to understand and appreciate the African view of the world and respect it as different from their own, but by no means inferior to it. Unfortunately, it is not possible, even in the twenty-first century, to claim that this healthy social interaction has been fully achieved. Also, and equally importantly, acknowledging and appreciating these differences can raise awareness for the African hosts, the very significant question as to what they, in turn, can learn from their guests' approach to the realities that are common to all humans.

This will be in line with the "both-and" inclusive approach to existence characteristic of Africans' own spiritual outlook, as elaborated in chapter five of this book. It is a spiritual stance, marked deeply by the readiness to accept and utilize whatever element that proves to be beneficial to human flourishing, regardless of its origin. The African's is a spiritual attitude that "consecrates relationality and maintains a clear distance from absolutism"—even cultural absolutism. Ultimately, it is a question of dialogue that is the winner in this process. Authentic dialogue between the two cultural outlooks will promote mutuality and cultural understanding. This is a much-needed commodity in our contemporary world, which is so much bound together in every way yet, paradoxically, is at the same time extremely divided and wounded, as never before.

It is impressive that from her relatively few years' observation as a guest in Africa—since 2008, to be exact—DiGennaro has written an extremely lucid and witty book about the pillars that sustain the African cultural heritage. At the same time, she provides insight into the philosophical mainstays of the West—how Westerners perceive and deal with life. These contrasting worldviews and convictions often disrupt understanding and performance in the economic, political, social, and spiritual-religious arenas. Here, in one relatively small volume, we have knowledge without which Africans and Westerners cannot expect to coexist—as friends, or merely as fellow human beings—in a world that increasingly compels people to rub shoulders with one another. The book cannot be recommended highly enough.

Laurenti Magesa, Ph.D. in Moral Theology
Scholar, professor, and author of several books, including
What is not Sacred?: African Spirituality.
November 2015, Nairobi, Kenya

Acknowledgements

For their interviews, I thank the many people who had tea with me—Africans, Westerners, and those who live somewhere in between. Your candid accounts ground this book and make it "real."

For reading my drafts as they emerged, immature and wobbly, thanks to Dr. Stephanie Black, Doris Diener, Donna Entz, Ibrahim Omondi, Jon and Jo Parsons, Jonathan Schlabach, and Andy Steere.

For turning concepts into illustrations, thanks to Debbi Omondi, my cousin and adult Third Culture Kid.

Mennonite Board, thank you for allowing me to invest time and energy in this project.

For guidance through the cycles of editing, thanks to the people at SIL International® Publications; Michael Jemphrey, Mary Huttar, and Eric Kindberg.

For a gracious Foreword, thanks to Professor Laurenti Magesa. Your fingerprints are all over this project, from your books, your lectures, and the material you shared in a personal interview over tea and samosas.

How this Book Works

In this book I articulate the African perspective on seven topics that I've observed to be most mystifying to Westerners in Africa: organization, finances, friendships, spirituality, communication and conflict, leadership, and work. In my own experience and observing other expatriates in Africa, I notice that we generally manage to adapt well enough to the food, the climate, sleeping under mosquito nets, and possibly even regular encounters with amoebas; but it's in the interpersonal dynamics where the battle for cross-cultural competence is won or lost, and these dynamics are commonly encountered at our places of work, worship, and recreation.

In the coming chapters I describe the African perspective and the Western perspective of these issues through a fictitious dialogue between a Western man, "Wesley," and an African man, "Juma." I have also included a number of true stories, either from my own experiences, from others' published accounts, or from the people I interviewed.

The people I interviewed turned out to be the real geniuses behind this project, generally not people with fancy credentials after their names, but those for whom cultural competence is a requirement for making their lives livable: people with a foreign spouse, the adult children of bicultural marriages, employees of foreign bosses, and adult Third Culture Kids who are, in their bones, at least as much African as they are Dutch, Canadian, or from wherever their parents originated. These people shared their stories with me, and have allowed me to share them with you, even though I have used pseudonyms to protect their identities.

At the end of each chapter I offer some questions to help readers reflect on what they have learned. The questions can be processed by an individual reader or as a group exercise. The questions are the same in each chapter, so they can be kept in the back of one's mind while reading. I also recommend related books that can help a reader go even deeper, if desired, with topics that are covered.

1

On Our Way to a New Culture

*Until the moment you go abroad, you have no reason or basis
for believing that other people, including foreigners,
might not behave like you.* (Storti 2007:68)

A matter of snakes

There was once a certain British man who went with his company to
Nigeria. He immediately noticed about Nigerians that the men did not step
back to allow ladies to enter a room ahead of them. This bothered him very
much. As a proper gentleman, whenever he approached a doorway at the
same time as a Nigerian woman, he courteously motioned for her to pass
through the door ahead of him.

After several months of this, he mentioned it one day to a Nigerian male
colleague. "Don't you know how impolite it is," he said, "to barge ahead of
a lady?"

His colleague looked at him strangely. "Sir," he said. "It's a matter of
snakes. The man must enter first so that, if there are snakes behind a doorway, he will get bitten but the lady will be safe."

This book is written for Westerners who want to develop cross-cultural
competence in for relating with African friends and colleagues. Cultural
competence is knowing what one needs to know in order to act in a manner

1

that is acceptable to the members of a given society. By behaving in acceptable ways, and correctly interpreting the behavior of others, we become socially mature in a given environment, worthy of trust, and able to engage new friends in genuine relationship.

Developing Cross-Cultural Competence

To become truly human is to learn a culture and understand what is going on. It is to know what to expect in life and what is expected of us.
(Hiebert 1986:57)

Most likely you are already very competent in one culture—your home culture—just like you are probably very fluent in your native language. Competency in a new culture develops much like the original competency did, through experience and the feedback of people around you.

Knowing what it is to understand and be understood in our own social environment, we desire to feel the same level of proficiency in new situations, whether relating to immigrants in our home country or traveling abroad. In this way, our established competency pulls us toward aptitude in new cultures. However, our established competency also has a pushing effect and can actually undermine our ability to perceive the world in new ways. As adults, our mental map of reality is firmly ingrained; only with difficulty can its marks and labels be re-drawn.

A foreigner sees only what he already knows.
(African proverb)

When we humans encounter new information, our brains run the information through a set of validity tests, checking it against what we already know. When the new information aligns with what we already know, with what we already recognize, we add it to our storage system. But if it does not ring true with the old data, the new data is quietly discarded. This process of validity-testing happens in a flash and usually below the level of our conscious awareness.

The British man saw Nigerian behavior, and navigating by European standards, thought he understood what was going on, when in fact he misunderstood completely. When the Nigerian courtesy was explained to him, he added new data to his storage system and afterwards was suddenly able to see and perceive the graciousness of behavior that had been there all along, invisible while in plain sight.

I am telling you about this process because I am hoping that, as you read this book, you can put your validity-testing process on pause. Just briefly. I am about to tell you some incredible things—things which are true but may not make any sense if you can test them only against realities you have experienced in your home culture. I am going to tell you that, although cows walk across the highways, and sometimes Xhosa people snip off the end of their children's pinky fingers, Africa's cultures are as normal as any other culture. Africa is organized, and its people behave in ways that are totally logical within their culture.

Redefining right-of-way

Traffic in Nairobi is notoriously maddening. Public buses lurch in and out of rows of bumper-to-bumper traffic, sometimes piled high with luggage and occasionally a chicken or goat. There appear to be no protocols for right-of-way, merging, passing, or slamming to a stop to drop off passengers.

One of the first questions I am asked by visiting Westerners is, "How ever do you manage to drive in this?" If traffic patterns in the United States went the way of Nairobi, it would indicate that something was very wrong.

In actual fact, driving in Nairobi is really quite predictable. The public buses are consistent in their lurching and slamming. Right-of-way is defined differently but reliably—basically, the biggest car goes first. Or maybe it's the most aggressive driver goes first. Actually, most of all, the protocol is "just don't get killed," which is a remarkably effective way to organize traffic.

It's not that there are no rules or traffic patterns; there are. But they look so different from what visitors are used to that they may not recognize them. Westerners can be so busy watching for what's familiar that they can't register the unfamiliar, unwritten system, and conclude that Nairobi's traffic has gone completely crazy.

Unfamiliar systems do make us uncomfortable. Freshly-arriving visitors to Nairobi clutch their car handles and turn pale; they are terrified; they are uncomfortable. But just because it's uncomfortable doesn't mean it's bad.

Foreigners in Africa, especially short-term workers, may be tempted to dismiss the importance of learning about African culture, eager to jump in and get to work. With any luck, we reason, real cultural differences are insignificant enough that they can be generally ignored. After all, we know how to be courteous: just let ladies go first.

Although a certain instinct may prompt visitors to minimize cultural differences, in fact, a greater appreciation of difference helps us forge a way forward. Notice what happens when we operate with the assumption that a person from another culture is basically like me: immediately my world and my experiences become central. To say that "we are basically the same," is to assume that the way I see things is the way they are.

This is the opposite of cultural competence. It is a projection. In attributing my own perspectives and feelings to others, I deny their reality. The assumption that other people are like us is, in fact, the source of most cross-cultural tension. Although it may feel backward, an honest recognition of other cultures and realities makes cross-cultural relationships more navigable, not less.

It turns out that one behavior can have different meanings. A behavior and its meaning are not one thing; they are two things—behavior and meaning. Letting ladies go first may be interpreted as kind, or as unkind. When we cross into a new culture, we will find that the people there may match behavior and meanings differently than we do. It is unnerving how local people interpret our behavior through their lenses, and not according to ours.

Competency in my home culture does not equal competency in other cultures, but by educating ourselves about another group's culture we can increase our likelihood of knowing what is going on and what is expected of us.

Establishing Credibility

Why does cultural competence matter? Because, as our saying goes, "When in Rome, do as the Romans do." That is to say, we adjust our behavior to fit the new context. It's easier on the "Romans," and ultimately, it's easier on us.

We expect no less of foreigners in our own countries. Consider the difference in your receptivity if a Somali woman dressed in Western clothes approaches you, speaking your language, and shakes your hand, compared with your receptivity to another Somali woman speaking Somali, dressed in a full black *abaya,* who is awkward with our style of greeting. It is easier to be receptive to foreigners who demonstrate behavior appropriate to our context.

Several days before a trip into Somalia, I had lunch with an American friend who was visiting Kenya. By way of conversation, I mentioned the preparations I was making for the Somalia trip, how I was practicing eating exclusively with my right hand, and had several new dresses sewn to meet the modesty requirements for women in a Muslim country.

"Why are you bothering with all that?" my American friend asked. "I think that people should accept me for who I am."

My trip schedule included an interview with the president of a university and the Minister of Education. "Well, I want my hosts to respect me," I explained. "I can't afford to do anything that will undermine my credibility."

"Oh," he exclaimed, seeing it in a new way. "It's an issue of *'When in Rome, do as the Romans do.'*"

Cultural Adjustment 101

The willingness to adjust to a new culture (rather than negate it) is essential for people who want to expand beyond the boundaries of their own ethnic group. There are some excellent books on the subject of adaptation; I have short-listed a few of my favorites at the end of this chapter. But for now, let me give a forty-five-second overview of the cultural transition process.

Basically, you've been marinating in your home culture since before you were born, and you're pretty well pickled. Whether we're aware of it or not, we have, in fact, been in culture school our entire lives, learning how to speak, work, joke, eat, and play with specifically coded cultural behavior.

Behavior that fits with a culture's written and unwritten rules is considered "right," "appropriate," and "reputable." Behaviors that break these cultural rules are considered "immoral," "devious," and "offensive."

This process of becoming oriented to a culture is called "acculturation." People groups have unique ways of enculturating their children; usually enculturation includes some form of punishment for "bad" behavior, and some form of reward for "good" behavior. Punishments can be things like physical spankings, bad grades in school, rejection, or gossip. Rewards may be praise, gifts, bonuses, promotions, and increased social status.

A person's worldview—the lens through which we view reality—is constructed during early childhood. As children transition toward young adulthood, their basic maps of reality "gel," and gradually become resistant to change. The validity filters solidify and become increasingly inflexible.

We then use our culture as the basis for evaluating other cultures. Ethnocentrism is a belief in the inherent superiority of one's own home culture. It's the assumption that the way my culture does things is the normal way, the best way. Now, this is totally natural. We all think our own way is normal. However, according to Duane Elmer (2002:59), "When we think we are *normal, we make a rather fatal slip into believing that we are also the norm.*"

Unfamiliar is Not Bad

We tend to evaluate other cultures, quite unintentionally, by their proximity to our own. If Canadian culture feels comfortable to me, I am likely to evaluate it as "good." If Chinese culture is very different and I end up feeling uncomfortable, I am more likely to evaluate it as "bad." That is to say, my evaluation of how good or bad something is has a great deal to do with the extent to which it is *like me*, the extent to which it fits with things I already know about.

This is an important factor to bear in mind as we engage with African cultures, because Africa is unlike the West in many and profound ways. We will encounter customs and values that are very unfamiliar and will need to guard against the natural inclination to assume that "familiar" equals "good" and "unfamiliar" equals "bad."

Anthropologist M. Herskovits defines culture as the human-made part of our environment (Whiteman 2015), including things like language, art, values, habits, customs, and so on. Every society has a culture. Much of what we do, while based on a biological need, takes form within a specific culture. For example, all humans need to eat, but the time of day I eat, whether I use a fork, chopsticks, or my hand, and my preference for pizza or *ugali* is largely determined by the culture in which I was raised. But relationships don't begin with biological similarities. Relationships start with relating. Meeting others and becoming friends is a social experience that always takes place within a cultural context.

> *All people see the same world, but they perceive it through different glasses.*
> *And they are often unaware of their culture and how it colors what they see.*
> (Hiebert 1986:52)

Although "most people believe their own assessments are correct and unbiased," says Lederleitner (2010:72), it's important to recognize that in actual fact, we all have a natural bias toward our own culture. A bias toward our own culture is, by definition, a bias *against* other cultures. This bias may become visible for the first time when we encounter another culture. "Until the moment you go abroad," says Storti, "you have no idea that what is normal to you is not also universal" (2007:68).

Culture Shock

We cannot underestimate how stressful it is, day after day, to face an environment that, as of yet, we do not know how to master. Culture shock is "a state of bewilderment and distress, experienced by an individual who is suddenly exposed to a new, strange, or foreign cultural environment."[1]

Or, as cross-cultural expert Duane Elmer describes it as, "Lost! That is the feeling of culture shock. You do not have the tools to navigate this new situation, and it is embarrassing, frustrating, frightening, and humbling" (2002:45). Although unpleasant, culture shock is a normal part of the process of adapting to a new environment.

Culture shock is caused, in part, by our own expectations. In preparing to go abroad most people have images of what it will be like, which, while cheerful, are usually flawed. Of expectations, Elmer (2002:54) says, "These gremlins hide in our pockets and sit unseen on our shoulders." Although we may not be aware of all our expectations, they are busy at work.

Two such expectation "gremlins" deserve special attention. Gremlin #1 is the expectation that other people are like us. We have discussed this already, but this belief runs deep and requires intentional effort to discard.

Gremlin #2 is the expectation that cross-cultural adjustment is going to go smoothly. "Cross cultural encounters don't always go wrong, of course, any more than same-culture interactions always go splendidly," says Storti (2007:25). "But, all other things being equal, they are certainly more likely to end badly." An expectation of ease quickly leads to early fatigue in the face of adjustment that is exhausting and humbling. Adaptation is neither casual nor cheap. Pry both of these gremlins off your shoulders as soon as possible and get on with the process.

A genuine relationship with Africa begins when we, foreigners and guests, see that indeed, that is what we are—foreigners and guests. We are no longer at home. When we quit expecting others to act like people do in our country, we are free to expect them to act like they do in their country. In our case, that means that we expect Africans to act like Africans. The people of Africa, in many ways, are not like us. They do not act like Europeans. They do not act like New Zealanders. African people are African. Whether the culture is easy or hard to adjust to, the onus is upon us, as the visitors, to adapt.

---

[1] Dictionary.com, http://dictionary.reference.com/browse/culture-shock?s=t. Accessed October 9, 2017.

Culture Clusters

As I've worked on this book many people have asked me about the wisdom of making general statements about the cluster of Western cultures and the cluster of African cultures. Neither region is homogenous. Germany, Canada, and Australia have unique cultures of their own and subgroups with distinct identities within their borders. Likewise, Africa is not homogenous either— South Africa, Burkina Faso, and Ethiopia are dissimilar in very substantial ways, including religion, language, economics, colonial histories, and so forth. There are fifty-four countries in Africa at the time of this writing and each country is home to a variety of distinct ethnic groups.

I acknowledge the unique cultures that exist within these broader clusters. For this study, however, I will speak in generalities about Africa and the West; if we were to zoom in too closely, we might drown in minutiae. A reader who is interested in ethnographic data on a specific group will want to locate materials that are specific to that group. In this text I take a bird's-eye view on the two culture clusters and attempt to build lines of comprehension and appreciation between them.

In speaking of the West, I am referring to the cultures of northwestern Europe, the United Kingdom, North America, and the Caucasian/ European populations of Australia, New Zealand, Israel, and South Africa— cultures heavily influenced at the core by scientific thought, some version of Christianity, and Enlightenment values (reason, analysis, and individualism). In speaking of Africa I am referring to the countries geographically south of the Sahara Desert. In spite of great diversity, these countries share some significant cultural foundations.

"But Africa is changing," you may say. And this is true. Cultures change, innovate and adapt constantly. The past fifty years have brought particularly astounding change to Africa, in terms of economic growth, health, education levels, and self-governance. Urbanization and globalization are changing the continent at internet speeds. More and more people are travelling for education and employment.

But—surprise!—Africa is still Africa. There is no greater way to honor other people than by entering into their world and living among them as they live. In this case, we are entering Africa, as it is, on its own terms.

The statements in this book are not guaranteed to be true of every African or Westerner at all times or in every circumstance. I can't predict my cousin

Joe's behavior with complete accuracy, not to mention the behavior of all of my countrymen. How much less could I impeccably predict African behavior! The statements are meant to describe typical cultural behavior, the way most things work, most of the time; as such, this book is a general guide for navigating African cultures.

Conclusion

The good news is that culture—the human-made parts of our environment—is learned. Babies learn culture from their families and communities and adults can learn it too. The bad news is that it requires time and effort. Even so, we will notice returns on even the small investment we make in cultural competence. Besides, if we aren't somehow intrigued by other cultures, wouldn't we just stay home in the first place?

Cross-cultural relationships can be likened to a marriage. Moving beyond the thrills of dates and daydreaming, the "real thing" is about learning to live with someone who has grown up in another family, with different ways of cooking, arguing, worshiping, and spending their money. A successful marriage is the result of two parties learning to forgive and communicate with each other, finding ways to enjoy each other in spite of real difference.

As a recent "in-law" to Africa myself—someone born to another family, but choosing to live in Africa—I would like to introduce you to what I have learned about the African family in our global village.

Questions for reflection

1. What did you learn from this chapter or think about for the first time?
2. Which of the African perspectives presented seemed the most different to you from your way of thinking?
3. When have you observed African friends' behaviors that connected with the observations in this chapter?
4. As a Westerner, what cultural mistakes do you think you may be most likely to make?
5. What ideas from this chapter would you like to discuss further with an African friend?

Recommended reading on cultural adaptation

Cross Cultural Connections: Stepping Out and Fitting In Around the World by Duane Elmer (2002). As a cross-cultural specialist, Elmer leads the reader through the basics of cross-cultural work. His emphasis is on building strong relationships through increased awareness, skills, and appropriate attitudes. Elmer's personal experiences in Africa tightly connect his work with the material from this book.

Cross-Cultural Partnerships: Navigating the Complexities of Money and Mission by Mary T. Lederleitner (2010). The author thoroughly examines the dynamics between donors and recipients—a must-read for people who are hoping to partner financially with African friends.

Cultural Intelligence: A Guide to Working with People from Other Cultures by Brooks Peterson (2004). This book helps the reader analyze components of culture, using scales of comparison (such as direct-indirect communication). These scales help us understand more about our own cultural styles, and how to apply cultural competence in the context of work and interpersonal relationships—relevant to those who are working with immigrants at home or traveling abroad.

Foreign to Familiar: A Guide to Understanding Hot- and Cold-Climate Cultures by Sarah Lanier (2000). This is a short and easy-to-read text that articulates the basic differences between cultures. Lanier's observations are relevant to Western and African encounters and beyond.

The Art of Crossing Cultures by Craig Storti (2007). Packed with practical insights, this book focuses on attitudes and skills for crossing cultures graciously. The style is humorous and light. This is my favorite on the subject of crossing cultures.

2

Clocks and Calendars: Navigating Concepts of Organization

Locals will assume that you understand their culture...and that you are knowingly behaving badly. (Storti 2007:87)

A wedding invitation

An African friend, Atieno, invited me to her daughter's wedding last year in Nairobi. On the day of the wedding, I drove my car to the outdoor venue where the wedding was to be, arriving right around the time I had been told the ceremony would begin. I was surprised to find that there were no other cars in the parking lot. The groom, who welcomed me warmly, the janitor, and I were the only ones on the property.

The next person to arrive was Joanne, a British woman, who apparently shared my proclivities for time, but she had been to many African weddings before and had the sense to stop on her way there for a cup of tea. Slowly, other guests began to trickle in and stood around chatting as they waited for things to get started. Eventually, the moderator of the ceremony found a microphone and began to entertain us with long introductions of honorable guests: grandparents of the bride and groom, pastors, and bishops. When he finished with that, he began to introduce them a second time.

The bride and her party, we were told, were stuck in a traffic jam, but that was just as well, because many of the guests were an hour or two late themselves (possibly stuck in similar traffic jams). When the bridal party did arrive, hours behind schedule, people took their places and the wedding began. No one was rushed, and no one apologized for the delay.

I don't know why I would expect an African wedding to be more or less like my own wedding, but for some reason, I admit, that expectation was in the back of my mind. My culture's rules about clock time and events are so deeply programmed into me that it was hard for me not to get anxious at that wedding, with so many things going "wrong," even though I was merely a guest and the hosts were not troubled at all.

Each culture has its way of handling time, schedules, and events. That is to say, the concept of organization and what it means to "be organized," is a product of culture and unique to specific environments. Africans order their time and events in distinctly African ways.

As with other concepts, the African definition of organization is hidden inside a culture's unwritten scripts. Although newcomers won't know conventions instinctively, they can learn about them, which is the purpose of this chapter. As we adapt, we will flow naturally toward genuine relationships and meaningful experiences.

Living with Ambiguity

A primary difference between African and Western concepts of organization is that Westerners believe, rightly or wrongly, that it is possible to control many aspects of life. We can, and we *should*. "Our American obsession with time and urgency leads us to want to schedule and control everything," observes Livermore (2006:60).

Juma: We assume we have a low level of control.

Wesley: We assume we have a high level of control.

Africans are more likely to believe, rightly or wrongly, that many of life's variables are outside of their control. This is sometimes referred to as "fatalism"—the belief that life's events are predetermined and therefore inevitable. Since many things lie in the hands of chance, or fate, there is no reason for people to assume they have a significant degree of ultimate control over their lives.

Although African people may be more fatalistic than Westerners, I contend that their environment is a key factor which strongly reinforces a sense of unpredictability. Although we Westerners may not fully appreciate it before we live in Africa ourselves, life in Africa is truly less "under control" than it is in the West. On any given day, there may be no water in the pipes, no electricity, a shortage of fuel, and all school teachers on strike. Instead of a problem, perhaps Africa's remarkable degree of flexibility is an adaptive measure for such an environment.

Imagine for a moment how it would feel to wake up tomorrow morning and discover that these factors would be part of your day. You can't do any kind of washing or bathing, all your devices are out of power, you can't drive anywhere, and your children are home from school.

This would change your day.

Many African people live continuously in this sort of *ad hoc* reality. If a day turns out to be very unlike what was expected, Africans assume that it's not a big problem or cause for blame; it's just the way things go. There are many variables we cannot control, but we make the best of whatever we have.

Events and the Clock

Our American obsession with time and urgency leads us to want to schedule and control everything. (Livermore 2006:60)

The appropriate time to start an event, by African standards, is when everything is ready—that is, the leaders of the event are set—things are arranged, and key people have arrived. The start time is not determined by the clock, which is seen as largely irrelevant, but by human factors, which are seen as significant.

Juma: Our events may start several hours after the advertised start time.

Wesley: Our events will probably start at the exact time advertised.

Events often start much later than the advertised start time, possibly several hours later, like the wedding I mentioned at the beginning of the chapter, which started three hours late because we were waiting for the bride. No one was upset by her delay; rather, it's obvious that a wedding can start only after the bride and her party have arrived.

It has been suggested, on behalf of Westerners, that we use the advertised start time as a rough guide for when to leave one's house (rather than be in one's seat). This is probably a fair rule of thumb (although there's no way to impeccably predict when an event will begin), but the simple reality is that there is no way to know exactly when an event will begin. When attending a wedding or similar event, it may be helpful to think of the whole day as being dedicated to that event. Err on the side of leaving your schedule too open, and take a good book (like this one!) in case of lengthy waits.

The pianist

I was told this story by Naomi, a North American woman who is married to a Kenyan man, and it illustrates how differently we understand what it means to arrive "on time."

"I had recently moved to Kenya, and agreed to play piano for the wedding of a couple from our church. The day arrived; I woke up early and got ready. The wedding was supposed to start at 11:00 a.m., and I knew I wanted to arrive half an hour early to make sure things were in order, which meant I should leave home around 9:30.

"By 9:00 I was nearly ready, but my husband was just crawling out of bed. Not wanting to nag, I tried to stay quiet, but when 9:20 rolled around and he was still brushing his teeth, I couldn't hold my panic any longer.

"'I am the pianist!' I snapped. 'I have to be at the wedding on time.' I was remembering another wedding in the United States where one person in the bridal party arrived late and the entire church crinkled and snapped with the tension of 150 people waiting for her. But my husband was unconvinced.

"By 10:00 I was fit to be tied, and my husband was still lethargic.

"By 10:15 I was in tears. If we left the house that moment and sped the entire way, I would arrive five minutes late.

"When we finally arrived at the church, it was 11:10. I sprinted across the parking lot and flung open the door to the sanctuary. But it was empty. No one else had arrived yet. Arriving slightly late, by North American standards, the pianist had arrived excessively early to the African event."

Juma: An event finishes when we have completed all the necessary parts.

Wesley: The clock determines when an event is done.

Events are not started by the clock, nor are they finished by the clock. The event is concluded when all the necessary components are complete. The particulars of what is needed depend on the type of event. For example, in ceremonial events (like weddings and funerals), there is a series of protocols to work through; in process events (like a community conflict resolution process) it is important that every voice be heard. We can assume that African people generally will not cut short events on the basis of time.

The same protocol applies when someone is giving a speech: a speaker will speak until he has delivered his message. Then he will stop. If the program says that Mr. Gitau will speak from 10:00 to 11:00 and then Mr. Kamau will speak from 11:00 to 12:00, this can be understood to mean simply that Mr. Kamau will speak *after* Mr. Gitau has finished. This is not upsetting to the African audience, and there is no social penalty for speaking longer than one's allotted time.

The priority of the event itself, over the time on a clock, makes sense when we consider that participants may have traveled a long way, possibly at personal expense, on uncomfortable public transportation, to attend the meeting. It is most considerate to run as late as necessary to finish a meeting's business at that time, rather than ask people to make a separate trip.

Planning

Africans usually formulate a plan at the time when they need it—that is, when a specific need arises; then they figure out what to do next.

There is a sense that the future is, in a way, not real. It doesn't exist yet. As an abstract and unknowable space, the future is not something to spend a lot of energy thinking or worrying about. Far-in-advance planning, then, is not particularly important or relevant.

For example, if an African friend is traveling to your town and needs a place to spend the night, he will probably call you within twenty-four hours of the time when he is hoping you can host him. Or he may not contact you at all and simply show up at your house. This "immediate planning" is not felt to be inconsiderate; it's just how things are done.

Juma: We make plans on the spot.

Wesley: We prefer to plan far in advance.

The African approach to planning can be a particular challenge for Western short-term visitors. Since we come from a culture that values planning in advance, we often spend hours and hours, writing up detailed trip itineraries months in advance, to meticulously fit the pieces together because our time will be short and we want the schedule to come out just right. Then we call our African hosts to confirm specific dates and times, and, being polite, they agree to the itinerary.

I would suggest that we understand this agreement to be more of a "why not?" than an official and definitive "yes." Even when Africans graciously bend to meet our need for advance scheduling, we should be aware that we are not guaranteed that everything will go precisely as we planned. The *modus operandi* for Africans is generally on-the-spot planning.

A North American woman, connected to the organization where I work asked me to help her arrange a workshop with the African group I work with. Her materials looked great, and I agreed to liaise between her and the local ladies. The first item on her agenda was to arrange a date for the workshop. The earliest she was available was eighteen months after our initial meeting.

"I'm not sure we can make concrete plans this far in advance," I said.

"But I have to fit it into my schedule," she insisted, "and I don't have a slot before then. Can you just ask the ladies if it will suit, and see what they say?"

"We can ask them," I said, "and they will say it suits. But the reason it 'suits' is because no one is thinking about what will be happening a year-and-a-half from now. If you want a solid commitment from them, we should wait until closer to the date."

Let's notice some components of the American's approach in this story "Get it on the schedule": After initiating a visit to Africa, she assumed that the planning would happen on her timetable. To some degree this is legitimate, in that the seminar can't happen without her; but when confronted with a discontinuity between her scheduling needs and her hosts' scheduling needs, she assumed that the African group would need to accommodate her.

It is so easy to assume that others need to capitulate to our way, which is, after all, normal. But as Storti (2001:88) says, although "it may not seem fair, the onus of learning how to behave in the local culture falls squarely on the guest, not the host." It's worthwhile to double check our expectations:

to what extent are we subconsciously expecting our hosts to capitulate to our concept of organization?

> **Juma: We are comfortable with ambiguous plans.**
> **Wesley: We prefer precise plans.**

Africans seem to feel most comfortable with plans that are pleasantly spacious. You will notice that African friends tend to make statements like, "I'll come over tomorrow," which is time-ambiguous, rather than "I'll come by 10:15," which is time-specific.

There is a sense that ambiguous plans are safer because there is room to encounter an obstacle, deal with it, retool, and still meet others' expectations. (Meeting expectations is very important.) On the other hand, precise plans set us up to fail. There is no way to accurately anticipate a day's obstacles. A schedule that is too tight, too defined, will probably end in disappointment.

This can be a trouble spot in Western-African partnerships because we want plans to be defined and clear up front (and may insist on it). If forced to comply with our preference for precision, Africans can certainly come up with a concrete plan, but that doesn't mean they actually buy into it.

We might protest that ambiguous expectations are easily exploited. That can be true; and particularly in a new situation or relationship, people can take advantage of unclear boundaries. (African people are not unaware of this and place the onus upon the owner to safeguard his resources.) However, although ambiguity can be exploited, ambiguity is not a problem in itself.

Suleiman's land battle

The following story illustrates the African preference for ambiguity, even in the context of a legal battle:

A Ugandan friend, Suleiman, was involved in a court battle over a piece of land for many years. At the beginning, the original owner agreed to sell the land to Suleiman for the equivalent of $2,500, which is about the amount Suleiman earned each year at his job. Over the next five years, he made a small monthly payment to the owner, eventually totaling about $1,000.

As time dragged on, the owner became impatient. He had hoped to get all the money up front, and to make matters worse, the property values in the area had increased significantly, and someone else was offering to buy it at a higher price.

When the original owner threatened to evict Suleiman, the case went to the local court. It was determined that the property value had doubled in those five years, and now Suleiman could either leave the land, or agree to a new price of $6,000.

Suleiman agreed to the new price.

It had taken Suleiman five years to pay $1,000, and without access to credit, it was unlikely that he'd be able to make larger payments than before. Even so, when the case left the court, the only thing they had agreed on was how much money he would pay. There was no agreement on monthly payments, or on the amount of time Suleiman had to come up with the full payment before the original owner had decided the property value has risen again.

Juma comments, "I imagine that Suleiman hopes the owner can be patient if he keeps up with monthly payments. The owner may stand to benefit from the situation, since he's getting good income while still owning the title to the property. And the judge probably doesn't want to bother with evicting Suleiman. So the ambiguous arrangement potentially benefits everyone."

Juma: Hope for the best, but don't count on it.

Wesley: We prefer realistic, accurate plans.

I observe that African people seem to live with an unruly blend of optimism and fatalism. While cheerfully hoping for the best in a given situation they may simultaneously be assuming that their plans will fail.

We Westerners, on the other hand, are not particularly interested in either optimism or fatalism but are most concerned that our plans are accurate. Hope, control, and good planning should be synchronized: they should advance simultaneously. Hope should not run ahead of careful planning and management.

In Africa, hope is a great virtue. Optimism is always appropriate; if nothing else, as a statement about one's confidence in God's goodness. It is generally considered inappropriate to dwell on pessimistic thoughts. For example, you might notice that your African friends rarely, if ever, plan for emergencies. This is connected in part to the taboos around discussing "bad" things, such as the possibility of someone becoming sick, or the disintegration of a business deal. Discussing a negative situation is seen, at a mystical level, as somehow calling forth that situation and feeding it energy. No one wants to increase the likelihood of bad things happening to them or to other people.

As Westerners collaborate with African people, we can be aware that Africans may be more inclined to optimism than we are and also more opposed, at some level, to trying to anticipate potential problems.

> **Juma: It's okay for plans to change.**

> **Wesley: Once plans are set, it is upsetting for them to suddenly change.**

Africans are remarkably flexible. I have observed African people responding to major adjustments with consummate graciousness and dignity, neither expressing distress nor casting blame on others.

People from the Western cluster of cultures may be less adept at improvising. Since we are accustomed to advance planning, we can be unnerved by arriving at a moment of our day and finding something different there from what we had expected. Particularly if we're already a bit tense, simply from the stress of operating in a different culture, a shift in plans can cause upset.

One cross-cultural worker suggested that to help Westerners keep their plans realistic, we should carefully write up our best-case scenario for the day, and then tear the paper in half. On a lucky day, we may be able to complete about 50 percent of what we're hoping for. Of course we can't know which of the lines on our script will actually not materialize, but it's probably fair to assume that many of them won't.

English class scramble

I took a team of English teachers into Somaliland for a week of English language classes. We were told that our first day would be only "ceremonial," consisting only of introductions between the teachers and students, but no class time. We confirmed this several times before we left our hotel to go to the school where we would be teaching.

We arrived at the school, we were introduced to the students as expected. And then our host said, "All right, you can all go to your classrooms for the next three hours." The teachers managed to keep straight faces long enough for the students to be excused, and then panic ensued. All of their lesson plans were lying on their beds at the hotel across town. No one had brought any chalk, pencils, or other teaching aids. We had no choice but to improvise the best we could.

Public Events

In the West, it is extremely important to arrive on time, if not slightly ahead of time. It is embarrassing to be late and considered disrespectful to other people. In some cases, it would be better not to go to an event at all rather than arrive there late.

Juma: We arrive when we can.

Wesley: Prompt arrival is obligatory.

In Africa, it is generally acceptable to "do your best" with arrival times. (After all, how can someone do *better* than his best?) If a meeting is scheduled for 1 p.m., the African participants will probably show up as close to 1:00 as they are able to. It may be 2:00 or even 3:00. There is a tacit understanding that delays are inevitable and we must excuse each other when someone's schedule is overtaken by events.

When conducting meetings with African colleagues, it is probably fair to expect that at least some of them will arrive late. Let's be realistic: it is going to happen. And when it does, resist the urge to make them feel guilty or press for an apology. Lateness does not equal disrespect in Africa and we should not treat it as if it does. When a colleague is delayed so long that you can't wait for him any longer, it is appropriate to call and ask him to reschedule the meeting, explaining politely that you need to move on.

Although Africans are generally quite permissive of delays, timeliness is important if you are meeting with a person of higher status than yourself. Although the high-status person himself is allowed to arrive late, people of high status do not expect to have to wait on people of lower status.

It is important that special guests be mentioned and possibly given a chance to address the audience. At a wedding, for example, the parents, grandparents, and other significant relatives may all be invited to speak to the audience. In a church service, it is common for the pastor to publicly name guests of high status and invite them to briefly address the congregation.

Juma: We like to publicly acknowledge our honorable guests.

Wesley: People are not usually called out of the audience, especially without forewarning.

Calling out guests is intended to honor them, and foreign visitors should be prepared to receive this honor. If I suspect that I may get a public introduction at an event, I prepare a few thoughts in advance, just in case, so I am not caught unaware.

The best response to a public introduction is to reciprocate honor, in some way, to our hosts. Several ways we can do that are to affirm the importance of the meeting or event, compliment the host or leader, and mention a special bond between yourself and the gathered group.

I encourage foreigners to be avoid using humor when making public comments. Jokes and plays-on-words are almost impossible to translate. I once heard an American woman make a humorous (but self-deprecatory) comment about being overweight. Her African translator hesitated, uncomfortable with the notion of insulting the guest speaker, then translated the word "overweight" as "healthy," which entirely changed what the speaker was trying to say. To avoid diminishing what you want to communicate, use language that everyone can understand.

Living in the Present

While Western culture tends to be oriented toward the future, African culture is oriented toward the present. Things that are actually happening now are most real and matter most.

Juma: The present is most real.

Wesley: But the future is most important.

In daily living, this present focus shows up as a preference for things that are actually happening now. For example, it would be unusual for an African to leave a meeting before it is finished because he needs to go to another appointment. The next appointment is not real yet, and who knows, it may not materialize at all.

Likewise, it would also seem strange if we Westerners excused ourselves from a meeting to leave for something else. Even if we are merely attempting to keep up with our schedule, it may send a message that we perceive the present event to be of less value than the coming one. We can honor our

African friends by living in the present with them—in our relationships, events, and organization.

Conclusion

African organization is not clock-centered and it's not efficiency-centered; in a word, African organization is human-centered. Organization revolves around maximizing the interconnectedness of the human community.

Just as I experienced at the tardy wedding, you will also probably experience discomfort, at times, with the ways that African friends and colleagues organize time. In those moments, when feeling bored, lost, overwhelmed, or frustrated by delays, we can bear in mind that negative emotions are a normal part of cross-cultural adjustment and don't necessarily mean we're doing something wrong.

In fact, as we participate in these unpredictable local events, we are probably doing something very right.

We will get the most out of African events when we keep our focus on relational priorities and do our best to forget about the clock.

Questions for reflection

1. What did you learn from this chapter or think about for the first time?
2. Which of the African perspectives presented seemed the most different to you from your way of thinking?
3. When have you observed African friends' behaviors that connected with the observations in this chapter?
4. As a Westerner, what cultural mistakes do you think you may be most likely to make?
5. What ideas from this chapter would you like to discuss further with an African friend?

3

Sharing, Hiding, and Hoarding: Navigating Concepts of Finance

To give to your friend is not to cast away; it is to store
for the future. (Swahili proverb)

A relay race

When my children were little, they attended a Kenyan preschool in Nairobi. On the last day of the year, the school hosted a "field day" with various competitions, one of which was a relay race where the children formed two teams and each child ran a segment of the race.

Early in the race, one team started to pull ahead of the other. Immediately, the teachers jumped in and began intercepting the runners on the winning team. Whenever one kid got a significant advantage over his opponent, the teachers literally picked up the little racer and held him in their arms until the other child caught up. At the end of the race, it was pronounced a "tie."

Kenyans are known to be world class runners so I assume that not all races are conducted this way. But the message that day to those children was clear: stay together, and adjust your pace to each other; this activity is for all of us.

The teachers' behavior caught my attention. They were far from being happenstance, I sensed that they were acting instinctively out of the values they themselves had learned as children in their home villages. In a situation where I expected a competition, they were behaving as communally-minded people. The experience helped me appreciate how pervasive this communal instinct is, even among the most modern, urban, and educated strata of African society.

Collective Thought versus Individual Thought

Dutch social psychologist Geert Hofstede (2004-2017a), drawing on research in more than seventy countries over forty years, created a measurement system for certain aspects of culture. One aspect he studied was individualism verses communalism. According to his research, the United States has the most individualistic culture in the world. On a score from 0 to 100, with 100 as most individualistic, Americans score a 91, closely followed by Australia (90) and the United Kingdom (89). In contrast, the African countries of Ghana, Nigeria, and Sierra Leone all scored 20, suggesting a strong preference for a collective approach.

Figure 3.1. Collective thought to individual thought index.

The seventy-point gap between African and Western cultures should catch our attention. Our cultures have programmed us very differently in this area.

As in other aspects of life, Africans tend to be more group oriented than Westerners in matters of finance. Families survive as a group, thinking primarily in terms of "us" and "ours" rather than "me" and "mine." The group is expected to care for the individual, and the individual in turn contributes back into the group, with no one person or family unit hoarding their resources for exclusive benefit. Interdependence is seen as normal and healthy. Although self-centeredness (individualism) is somewhat instinctual, it is likely to be interpreted as a childish trait, something that mature people have learned to tame, and ultimately to replace, with altruism for the collective.

Keep the image of the school children in your mind as we discuss finances—it may help form an intuitive connection to the African concept of money management. Just like in that relay race, the financial aspect of life is not seen as an individual activity. Ideally, those who are able to run ahead should adjust for those whose strongest suits lie elsewhere. The highest goal is that the collective group makes it to the end, together, and with their dignity in place.

Bad apples

One caveat before we jump in: Every society has its share of what my grandmother used to call "bad apples," that is, malicious people who exist among the majority of otherwise reasonable, honorable people. Our Western culture has them and so does Africa.

When working in another culture, however, we are not always good at differentiating the "bad apples" from the upright majority who are merely acting according to their cultural norms (instead of ours). Since we can be particularly uptight around matters of money, we must take extra care to refrain from projecting our norms onto others. When our new friend breaks the "rules," it's usually because he is operating with a totally different set of rules, which he also assumes is normal for us.

Both the Western and the African systems have weaknesses, and plenty of incidences could be cited where both have broken down. Our purpose here is to learn about the African system, because learning—even if the new system doesn't feel natural—is the first step to building cross-cultural competence.

Living in community

> **Juma: Our system is set up to provide a basic level of survival for the many members of a group.**
>
> **Wesley: Our system is set up for individuals to accrue as much wealth as they can.**

In African cultures, wealth is viewed as a liquid which should naturally cover a given space, in spite of higher and lower points along the bottom. If one person or family unit has higher earning power, they are expected to let some of their wealth "flow down" to members of their extended family system who have lower income or earning power.

By leveling out the resources, this system is meant to provide a basic level of survival for all the members of a group. No one in the family circle becomes excessively wealthy, but hopefully, no one will become totally destitute either. There is a strong sense of security that comes from being part of a group with regular habits of give-and-take.

In contrast to the Western capitalist system, where everyone tries to accrue as much for himself as he can, the African system, in its ideal form, prioritizes the survival of the community. Tanzanian professor and author Laurenti Magesa refers to this as the African philosophy of "eating together"—that is, literally eating together, often from a common pot, as well as figuratively "eating together" by living in solidarity as a community through times of plenty and lack. He says, "The African economic perspective, based on the philosophy of 'eating together,' emphasizes mutual dependence and cooperative success above competition and individual accomplishment in economics as in every activity" (2013b:150).

Your success is my success

Sometimes an extended family system realizes they can't afford to put all of their children through school. Instead, they may agree together to invest in one or two of their more promising members. Pooling their resources, they help that person complete his or her education.

Eventually that person will finish his education, get a job, and begin to earn a paycheck. After years of his family's investing in him, his success legitimately belongs to everyone. They have built him up to a level beyond where he could have reached on his own and now he is duty bound to build up the larger system in return.

Investing in the family system often takes the form of helping to pay for siblings' education, helping adult siblings to pay for their children's education, supporting aging parents, and making significant donations for family events (funerals, weddings, and other ceremonies).

Juma: The line between your things and mine is ambiguous.
Wesley: The line between your things and mine is very clear.

In the community where I grew up, everyone had his own possessions. American children take their *own* toys to the beach. College students buy their *own* textbooks. And if someone forgets his own sunscreen lotion at the park, he'll probably burn before he asks to borrow lotion from a stranger.

We are not culturally programmed to expect to share as extensively as Africans do. In the African context, very few belongings, if any at all, are exclusively owned by an individual person. Possessions are meant to be used, not hoarded, and they are meant to be used by "us."

This means that Africans assume they are allowed to use the resources and belongings of others, at least to a greater extent than Westerners usually would. The more closely one is connected to another person, the more entitled he is to that person's things. For example, my African friend Njeri explains, "I can go to my brother's house and use whatever he has that I need, even if he is not at the house."

As we get closer to African friends, it is likely that they will show an interest in sharing some of our belongings. Sometimes they may ask permission first; other times they may assume they are free to borrow without asking. From our cultural definition of friendship, a Westerner may feel that his African friends do not respect his belongings—since we show respect by leaving someone else's things alone. However, from the African's cultural perspective, anything less than enthusiasm to share, by the Westerner, may be interpreted as a lack of respect for the relationship, since a true friend would never be miserly with what he has.

We consciously think about boundaries in many of our relationships, and cross-cultural friendships are no exception. Among Africans, there are significant expectations for sharing, and the Westerner who can develop fluency in this system will demonstrate profound solidarity.

Unintentional "Sharing"

The onus is upon the owner to safeguard his belongings if he does not want them to be considered available to others. Safeguarding usually includes hiding items or keeping them under lock and key.

"You have to put restraining measures in place or things will always disappear," Njeri told me. "You have to come up with ways to control the items in your house."

Secondly, if it comes to our attention that one of our belongings has "walked away," we must proceed carefully. A belligerent or blaming response will be interpreted as petulance. Moreover, we quickly make enemies if we overtly blame a specific person for the problem.

In the unfortunate situation that something has disappeared, and there doesn't seem to be a way to retrieve it without rupturing relationships, I recommend that the owner consider the item lost and focus his energy on developing culturally appropriate safeguards for the future.

Friendship and Sharing

In the African system, goods and finances which are not needed for today's survival can be claimed by relatives and close friends. Why should one family hoard a surplus, while a relative's family goes hungry?

Juma: Resources I am not presently using are to be shared with family members and close friends.

Wesley: I have money that I won't spend today, but it's still mine to keep.

Anything that is not immediately being used or cared for by someone is seen as "surplus" goods. Surplus goods can be food, tools, cash, appliances, and miscellaneous supplies—really anything that is left lying around. The logic is that, if the owner had needed this item, he would not have left it unattended. If he does not need it, then it is a spare item that can be legitimately claimed by someone who does need it.

Unattended "surplus" items, I should add, have a remarkable way of disappearing.

Helping oneself to surplus items is not necessarily seen as stealing, although Westerners may initially interpret it to be. Lederleitner observes, "In individualist cultures, stealing is defined as taking a possession that belongs to another person and using it for our own personal benefit without the owner's prior consent. [In communalist cultures] any resource already belongs to the entire community. If it is not being used by the current owner, it is allowed to be borrowed and used by others at any time" (2010:42).

> **Juma comments, "We don't always like our own system; it can cause much inconvenience, but we assume that it's more or less how things go."**

Foreigners in Africa, often perceived to be wealthy, get frequent requests for loans and other donations (as do wealthy Africans). Over time, these requests can be overwhelming. The balance between generosity and genuine financial limitations can be a tedious spot to find.

Culturally Competent Sharing

- You don't need to take a request too seriously if it comes from someone you don't know personally (such as a colleague who is raising funds for his cousin's wedding). A small token gift, perhaps something worth about two packages of sugar, is quite adequate.
- You don't need to supply the entire amount requested. The petitioner is probably raising funds among his whole circle of friends. It is fine to chip in a portion of the total amount.
- Aim to give in ways that are congruent with what a local person, in a position similar to yours, would give. We want to contribute approximately the same amount as others, neither giving much more nor much less. (A gift that is too large or too small may convey an additional message that you don't mean to send.) By giving a standard amount, we communicate solidarity without promoting unhealthy dependency. If you're unsure of what an appropriate amount would be, talk to a trusted local friend or culturally competent expatriate.
- It is helpful to decide your boundaries in advance. If you have a spouse, it is likely that one person is more open-handed than the other, so be sure to define this boundary together.
- If you must turn down a request, do so with diplomacy. A direct "no" is often seen as a tactless, or even a childish, way to communicate with another adult. In chapter 5, we will look more deeply into concepts of cross-cultural communication.

Friendship and Money

Westerners are suspicious of a friendship that involves financial or material exchanges. Real friendship, we believe, is based on an emotional connection between people. People should be friends because they like each other, not because they hope for something to gain from the other person.

The African concept of friendship is quite different. Africans believe that a relationship is strengthened by connections of various types—social connections, maybe ethnic connections, and financial connections. Sharing resources is a primary way of showing that you are more than a "fair weather" friend. One African proverb says, "Brotherhood does not mean physical resemblance, but mutual assistance." That is to say, mutual assistance defines a friendship. Mutual assistance creates and confirms loyalty in relationships.

> **Juma: If I need money I can ask family members and close friends; financial transactions strengthen relationships.**

> **Wesley: It would be awkward to solicit money for my personal use from friends and family; financial transactions between friends sour their relationship.**

Westerners generally do not think of friends as sources of credit. If someone needs a loan, it would be more common to put a purchase on a credit card or take out a loan from the bank, but it's considered poor taste to ask friends to make a donation. We expect people, ideally, to live within their means and provide for themselves.

In contrast, Africans think of friends and family members as legitimate sources of gifts and loans. It is perfectly appropriate to raise money among colleagues at work, friends from church and employers, especially for unusual or unforeseen expenses which are too much for the average person to meet on his own.

When an African friend invites you to get involved with him financially, it is very important to consider your level of commitment to that relationship. A token gift, appropriate in quantity for the social context, is adequate for a casual friend, but a close friend deserves something more. The way you respond to his request sends a message about your commitment to the relationship. Be generous, but don't communicate a deeper commitment than you are able to follow through with. We will look more deeply into concepts of friendship in chapter 4.

> **Juma: We take it as a compliment when someone asks for money.**

> **Wesley: We feel uncomfortable when someone asks for money.**

When Africans ask each other for help, the underlying message is something like this: "I perceive you as a generous person," or "I see that you have done well for yourself," or "I want to have a closer relationship with you." These are compliments, or at least they are generally perceived as positive messages, regardless of whether the donor is able to give what the asker requests.[1]

Quite the contrary is true when foreigners in Africa are asked for money. We generally don't feel flattered; we feel awkward and sometimes even angry. When a new African friend requests money, says Maranz, and the request comes before a sense of mutual respect and cohesion has been built, the Westerners perceive this as an attempt to buy his friendship, or manipulation (2001:66).

We can anticipate that African friends will act according to their cultural norms, regardless of how we feel about financial requests. I don't suppose I will ever get to the point that I actually enjoy being asked for money, but, if we hope to develop friendships with Africans, we must train ourselves to handle such situations graciously. Remember, we are not obligated to be the neighborhood ATM; but we are obligated to be courteous.

On loans and loyalty

For Westerners, a loan is a specific type of financial transaction whereby something is borrowed with the expectation that it will be paid back, possibly with interest. However, I have observed Africans using the word "loan" quite differently. When "loaning" money to each other, Africans seem to have an understanding that the loan may be repaid through non-material avenues, such as a deepened friendship, an increased sense of loyalty, or by the borrower contributing generously the next time the lender has a need. As we understand loans, it may never be paid back at all. "Many people live with debts they don't expect or intend to ever repay," says Maranz (2001:155).

> **Juma: A "loan" between friends is, most likely, a gift.**
>
> **Wesley: A loan is totally different from a gift.**

When the loan comes due (if a due date was determined), it is generally seen as the duty of the lender to go find the borrower and ask for his money. The borrower probably won't bring the payment voluntarily. If the borrower is unable to repay his loan at that time, the lender, ideally, will be lenient and agree to extend the time without making a scene.

---

[1] Maranz (2001:129) confirms this difference in attitude between Africans and Westerners.

When the lender is clearly on a higher economic level than the borrower, as most foreigners are perceived to be, actual repayment becomes even less likely. It is seen as poor taste for a wealthy lender to demand repayment from a poor man, for obviously the poor man faces many more disadvantages than the wealthy one, who had the surplus money to lend out in the first place.

Lederleitner explains of communal cultures, "Everyone knows that if a less affluent [person] delays paying back a loan to a wealthier [person], the wealthier person will be patient and understand. He or she would never confront or put pressure on the poorer family member, for to do so would cause shame and create disharmony in the relationship" (2010:41).

If the lender eventually "forgets" the loan altogether, it indicates that he is a generous person, and that he has the maturity to value his relationship with the borrower above the money he "invested" in the situation.

Given the relaxed attitude toward repayment, Westerners in Africa may get closer to the conceptual target if we think of a "loan" as a euphemism for what we otherwise understand as a "donation." There are some African people who will repay a loan in the way we expect, but there are also many who will not.

Paying ahead

Westerners prefer impersonal systems for investment and savings. We feel secure when we have money—the more, the better—stashed in our bank accounts, retirement accounts, pension plans, and investment portfolios. American financial guru Dave Ramsey (2003) recommends that people hold enough money in their savings accounts to survive for 3–6 months without income. All our accounts and investments ensure that we will never get into a position where we have to ask friends and relatives for financial help.

> **Juma: The best way to save for the future is to financially collaborate with family and friends.**
>
> **Wesley: The best way to save for the future is to build my portfolio.**

In contrast, African people typically do not stash away money for the distant future. Rather, the most common way that Africans save money is by "paying ahead." Give a cousin a gift today, and the next time you are in need, he will be obligated to give you a gift in return. With wise and continuous investment over one's lifespan, a person can accrue favors and "credit" throughout a broad network of friends, relatives, and clansmen.

"This arrangement constitutes a virtual banking or savings system," says Maranz (2001:26). Working as a safety net, the web of friends and relatives provides security for each other. A sense of security comes—not from stockpiling resources for one's self—but from participation in a community that is committed to you for life.

Open Air Markets

Many visitors love to shop in Nairobi's open-air souvenir markets. The Maasai Market, as it is called, has scores of vendors that sit in rows, displaying their baskets, cloth, wooden bowls and soapstone carvings on colorful blankets that serve as their "shops."

Foreigners are easy to spot, and their "easy money" attracts a lot of attention from vendors. The vendors generally assume that tourists are wealthy (at least wealthy enough to take international vacations) and that they are likely to be unfamiliar with standard market prices. With this in mind, I have heard vendors quote tourists "opening prices" that are inflated to 500 percent of the actual price. Of course the tourists could get their items for reasonable prices, but they would have to be able (and willing) to do the work of bargaining. Quite often, they pay the stated price or simply forego the item.

If you plan to go to the open-air markets, think about what you might want to buy ahead of time. Talk with local friends about standard costs so you know what prices you're going to aim for. Be sure to allow enough time in your plans to interact with the sellers; bargaining takes a lot more time than pulling an item off a shelf.

Ways of giving

A Canadian friend I met in college, a man named David, grew up as a missionary kid in Burkina Faso. Reflecting now, as an adult, on his interactions with African peers, he comments: "When [my African friend] gave me a gift—a slingshot, a sack of oranges, a basket of peanuts—I thanked him warmly and considered the matter closed. I didn't imagine that these gifts might be small investments he hoped to collect on someday."

David continues, "When my friends asked for money, they weren't being rude; they were giving me opportunities to invest in social capital. These requests belonged to a system of social security in a world without banks, credit cards, or insurance agencies" (Neufeld 2013:43).

In the West it is possible (and common) to make a one-time charitable donation to an organization; you send a check; they send a thank-you note, and that is the end of the transaction.

> **Juma: A material exchange enters us into an informal contract with another person.**
>
> **Wesley: I can give a one-time gift without implying a long-term commitment.**

In Africa, however, giving gifts is usually a social transaction, as well as a financial one. When someone contributes to a person or cause, it is a way of "signing up" and "joining in." Why would you invest in something and then walk away from it?

Although generosity is commendable, the Western way of "disinterested" giving sends an ambiguous message. For example, I met an American woman on her two-week trip to Kenya. During her visit, she found an orphanage that really moved her. She decided to donate a large sum of money to it—about $15,000. In spite of her good intentions, she was completely oblivious to the message she was sending with a gift of that size; to the African recipients, she was initiating an extremely deep relationship, and yet her plan was to write a check and walk away.

"What is it like," I asked my Kenyan friend, Achieng, "to be in a friendship with Westerners?"

"It's very confusing!" she admits. "Someone acts like a close friend, but then...." Her voice trailed off.

Messages (including unintended messages) of commitment, when coupled with the expectation of a disinterested relationship, set the stage for frustration and hurt. I recommend that foreigners who want to give, do so "softly." It is wise to share with our African friends in a way that doesn't imply a level of commitment that we don't intend. Generosity is a good thing, but it must be congruent with our intended level of relationship.

Negotiations

In the West, we can get quotes for goods and services. If you need to know how much the local lawn service costs, you call them and ask. Prices are usually set, regardless of who you are or who picks up the phone when you call.

Juma: Always expect to negotiate.

Wesley: Most service providers have fixed prices.

In Africa, prices are contingent on many variables and usually are open to negotiation. A service provider's opening price will be partly dependent on how well he knows you and how wealthy he judges you to be. (People with greater means are generally expected to be willing to pay more than common people, observes Maranz (2001:127).) It is appropriate to ask for quotations, but they may be negotiable. Bear in mind that another person in your social circle may be able to get significantly different prices than you can.

Be aware that full payment closes a business negotiation. After the buyer pays, there is no further room to negotiate; any addendum or adjustment will be considered a new transaction. If possible, make a deposit, but hold full payment until the service is delivered according to the agreement.

I recommend that we think of negotiation as a sort of social chess game. The buyer and seller sizing each other up, the first offer and counter offers, the banter, the dialogue—negotiation is a competitive, social activity. It's about much more than the bottom line. Should the "game" get frustrating, stay calm. Any show of anger or impatience will only give the other party the upper hand. Check your strategy, and keep negotiating.

Getting the right price

I hired two men to do a small construction project on my home in Nairobi. At the outset, we agreed that I would pay them the going daily rate. "Does that include lunch?" I asked.

"That's our flat fee," they replied.

But when I came to check on them the next day, I realized that they left the worksite for the day at 3:00 p.m. I wasn't sure how to interpret what was happening. Do they usually work short days? Are they trying to exploit the situation? Or perhaps they just hadn't thought about how and when they would eat lunch.

The following day I approached the foreman calmly and explained my concern. After a bit of dialogue, we were able to renegotiate and find a solution that satisfied both of us.

Juma: It is a buyer's responsibility to know the reasonable cost of an item at the market.

Wesley: It is the seller's responsibility to calculate a reasonable price.

When an African goes to the market, he knows the approximate cost of the items he intends to buy. Since prices probably won't be marked—and it is assumed the seller will make as much profit as he can—the buyer needs to know approximate costs so he can advocate for himself in the bargaining.

Admittedly, this tag-less system puts visitors, who are unfamiliar with local prices, at a disadvantage (not to mention the extra strain of purchasing in a foreign currency.) When it's possible, I personally prefer to shop in stores where prices are marked. However, the interaction that comes through bargaining can help us learn or practice what we already know, about the language and culture. Moreover, it may be the only way to buy things in rural areas. It's impossible to bargain well without knowing standard market prices, so confer with your African friends about reasonable prices before you leave home.

(Incidentally, it may also be the buyer's responsibility to have change; shopkeepers often don't have any on hand.)

Handling requests for borrowing

Since sharing resources is ubiquitous in Africa, it is important to understand the expectations of lending practices. When it comes to goods being swapped back and forth, it is the lender who carries the risk of her items being lost, damaged, or simply kept.

Juma: Liability is carried by the lender.

Wesley: Liability is carried by the borrower.

If you loan your neighbor a computer, and it breaks while he has it, you are responsible (as the owner of the computer) to pay for its repairs. If your neighbor could afford a computer, he would probably own one himself. The borrower may also keep the computer until you specifically come to his house to ask for it back.

Sometimes a friend asks to borrow something that, in light of the risks, we are not comfortable sharing. Africans of means face this dilemma as well and have to navigate between the potential social cost of refusing a request and the financial cost of losing a belonging. In such a situation, my goal would be to hang on to the item while managing the situation in such a way that does not offend or insult the asker.

There are many ways to do this, but let me mention two of the more common ones. First, you can give an external reason why you are unable to give the loan. It's not that you don't want to help, it just isn't possible right now for some reason: "I wish I could lend you my computer, but it is in the shop." This is a polite and acceptable way of declining the request.

The second way to deal with unwelcome requests is to simply keep special items hidden. Some wealthy Africans keep secret their bank accounts, property titles, certain assets, or other items of value, as a way of protecting themselves from obligations to share or "loan."

Although it's normal to "lend" items when you are able to, the volume of requests can exceed our financial limitations. Again, I highly recommend that Westerners think ahead about how to handle requests. We want to share with friends; we also want to avoid unhealthy relationships.

The wedding car

One of our employees was planning his wedding, and he requested to use our Prado as the wedding vehicle. We knew that his wedding was taking place in one of Nairobi's slum areas, where the roads can be very hard on a vehicle, and also we didn't know who would ultimately sit behind the wheel, so we were not comfortable with the idea. Nevertheless, we wanted to be diplomatic because we valued the relationship with this employee, so we explained that we wanted to help him, but we needed the Prado on that day for a trip upcountry. Could we perhaps help with the cost of a taxi instead?

Although, factually, we did not have plans to go on a trip that day, we felt like it was a socially acceptable way to decline the request while honoring the relationship.[2] The issue was quickly settled, and both of us were satisfied with the outcome.

Juma: Immediate needs get priority.

Wesley: Resources should be budgeted and saved for future expenses.

As a rule, "people [in Africa] expect that money and commodities will be used or spent as soon as they are available," says Maranz (2001:16). The first need that presents itself gets priority. A bill that's due today is of greater concern than the rent payment that's not due until next week. Tomorrow is another day.

A taxi driver friend in Nairobi reports that the city roads, usually choked with traffic, become much less congested at the end of the month. "It's the end of the month," he shrugs, "people are out of money."

Salaries are usually paid in the first week, and as bills come due and purchases are made throughout the month, earnings get whittled away. By the last week of the month, there are enough drivers who can't afford to fuel up their vehicles that we all get a break from the traffic jams until pay day comes again and the roads turn back into a zoo.

This is not necessarily a matter of fiscal carelessness. It's a different way to organize spending, in a context where money often can't be stretched quite far enough, and people survive the weeks by cleverly outwitting poverty.

Juma: Precise accounting should be avoided; it indicates mistrust between parties.

Wesley: Precise accounting is the bedrock of any respectable business endeavor.

Accounting

In the West, we believe that accurate accounting is important, and that individuals and society at large are protected by truthful and reliable records. In Africa, asking to see precise financial records hints of suspicion. When someone questions the way another person handles funds, it may be interpreted as a lack of trust. Out of a desire to live in a spirit of understanding

---

[2] Be sure to see chapter 6 on communication, where I discuss the importance of saving face (maintaining honor) in dialogue and conflict.

between people, Africans are more likely than Westerners to shrug off financial miscalculations when they occur.

Although culturally competent Westerners should not give up on accounting, we can be aware that our African friends may not be as open or precise about money management as we would expect from our countrymen. Here are several suggestions to help us stay ahead of common trouble spots:

Staying Ahead of Receipting Trouble Spots

- Familiarize yourself with prices. If I hire a plumber to fix a pipe, I myself should have an idea of the cost of the pipe. I can also ask the plumber about prices, but it is not considered unethical for him to use my ignorance to some slight advantage of his own.
- Don't expect change. When you send the plumber to the store to buy parts, try to give him, as much as possible, the exact amount of money he needs rather than a larger sum; the general expectation is that if there is change left over it will belong to him as a sort of tip.
- Don't blindly rely on receipts; they are only moderately useful. Receipts in the marketplace are usually handwritten (not computer generated) so is easy to take advantage of the system. If you send someone to the market to make a purchase on your behalf and the buyer knows the seller—which is likely—they can agree on how much a receipt should be written for. An American in West Africa recounts, "After paying a well-known doctor in a major city for a consultation, I asked for a receipt. He responded nonchalantly, 'In what amount?'" (Maranz: (2001:191). When reimbursing someone on the basis of a receipt, it is wise to be informed about local market prices, and take the time to occasionally verify documentation.

Ideally, we will learn to relate to people in a big-hearted and trusting way, while simultaneously exercising enough common sense to keep them trustworthy.

Reimbursement for work shoes

In our first year of managing a guest house in Nairobi, my husband and I decided to give our staff a new benefit, whereby the company would provide a high-quality pair of shoes for each employee to use at work. After checking around the local shops, we agreed to pay a certain amount for shoes. We asked employees to select a pair that fit his or her feet, was appropriate for his or her department, and was agreeable to them, and we would reimburse receipts up to (the equivalent in shillings of $18).

We were surprised when every single person returned with a receipt for exactly $18. No one brought a receipt for one shilling less or one shilling more. One woman even got two pairs of shoes for a total of exactly $18.

We quickly realized our mistake. We had given employees a chance to "earn" extra money: by purchasing a cheap pair of shoes that they could tolerate at work, and then possibly adjusting the receipt, they were able to pocket the rest of the money we reimbursed. I doubt that everyone took advantage of our flimsy system, but we certainly invited policy abuse by the way we handled receipts. The next year, of course, we created a tighter system.

One-pocket system

Westerners expect that funds belong to the owner or donor and must be used only for the intention of that person or entity. From our perspective, redirecting that money is thievery and can be prosecuted by law.

> **Juma: We often have "one pocket" for personal and organizational funds.**

> **Wesley: We have "two pockets": personal money is totally different from money I manage on behalf of someone else.**[3]

A "one pocket" system implies an absence of separation between money that belongs to a person privately and monies that he directs on behalf of someone else. In Africa, a person who is entrusted with money or other resources expects to have a major say in how it is used. That person, the manager, has some right to direct the funds according to his own assessment of priority.

---

[3] Maranz 2001:141–142

There may be times when the manager will elect to utilize funds in a way that benefits his group or even benefits him personally. This is one of the perks of being in management or of having a member of your group in management. It seems that, as long as the manager doesn't get excessive with this benefit, people generally shrug it off as normal.

Combine this expectation, leniency in accounting, and a cultural preference to avoid confrontation, and it's not hard to imagine how things can get tricky when Westerners give or loan money to African partners. When our expectations are violated, it feels very much like a breach in ethical behavior. Although there definitely are scammers who want to exploit donors (just as there are in our countries), not every African who handles money differently from us should be considered an embezzler. They may be working well within the ethical expectations of their context. In fact, Africans see their approach as being *pro-family:* they bring benefits home to one's own family and community, rather than siphoning benefits away to a distant corporate entity who is probably operating with huge surpluses anyway.

Conclusion

The practices of mutual dependency are not only normal among Africans, as well as immensely practical, they are viewed as markers of social maturity and moral character. Magesa says that sharing is an act of prayer, which acknowledges that the primary owner of all possessions is God (2013b:86).

Remember the relay race from the beginning of the chapter? African children are taught early the behavioral codes of altruism. Although it is very different from our system, and certainly no less flawed, I hope we can recognize the mutuality of the African system as an essential part of the African genius.

Questions for reflection

1. What did you learn from this chapter or think about for the first time?
2. Which of the African perspectives presented seemed the most different to you from your way of thinking?
3. When have you observed African friends' behaviors that connected with the observations in this chapter?

4. As a Westerner, what cultural mistakes do you think you may be most likely to make?
5. What ideas from this chapter would you like to discuss further with an African friend?

Recommended reading on finances

African Friends and Money Matters by David Maranz (2001) is a thorough discussion of important differences between Western and African perspectives on money. Written by a missionary anthropologist, this book draws heavily on his several decades of personal experience in West Africa. If you are interested in going a step further with the ideas from this chapter, *African Friends* is a must-read.

Cultural Partnerships: Navigating the Complexities of Money and Mission by Mary T. Lederleitner (2010) focuses on the dynamics of engaging in financial partnerships with international partners. The author explains how cultural differences can cause tension when Westerners get involved with people in other parts of the world. This text is a guidebook to successful cross-cultural partnerships. Don't enter a partnership without it.

When Helping Hurts: Alleviating Poverty without Hurting the Poor...or Yourself by S. Corbett and B. Fikkert (2009) is a compelling argument about the ways in which people with good intentions sometimes exacerbate the very conditions they are trying to alleviate. The authors unpack some of the assumptions behind our notions of helping the poor, especially for "helpers" who are going from wealthy countries to Majority World countries. By contrasting relief, rehabilitation, and development, they assist the reader in clarifying and evaluating which approach is appropriate for a given situation.

4

Allies and Obligations:
Navigating Concepts of Friendship

If there's one thing nearly everyone who lives and works abroad has to get right, it is this: they must be able to get along with the local people.... And yet a great many expatriates cannot. (Storti 2007:xv)

Relationships and Reciprocity

When executing a cross-cultural move, we need the comfort of friends more than ever. Unfortunately, it is at this very moment when old friends are far away, and new friends seem curiously unavailable, that we feel stuck behind the glass window of culture. Considering how elemental the need for friendships is, it's surprising how few expatriates manage to find a way around the glass window and actually develop meaningful friendships with local people.

In Africa, we are pushed apart by the forces of colonial histories, skin color, language, and perceived economic disparity. However, I would contend that more powerful than these forces are our differences regarding the concept of friendship that create the biggest obstacle.

When we Westerners think about our relationships, we often think in terms of how much we like a person. When deconstructed, the degree to which we like someone usually pertains to our shared interests, ease in relating to each other, and other emotional components. We might describe friendships in the West as *recreational*, meaning that we primarily understand friendship in terms of enjoyment and emotional satisfaction.

African friendships, on the other hand, are much more practical. To explain the African concept of friendship to Westerners, I prefer to use the term "ally." An *ally* is someone with whom we cooperate for a purpose. It is possible to have a warm emotional bond with an ally, but that is a perk; the basis of the relationship is commitment to a shared purpose. In the African concept of friendship, our friends are our allies. We depend on each other's practical help in the epic struggle for survival.

With culturally specific understandings of what is at the core of friendship, we should not be surprised that genuine cross-cultural friendship takes considerable effort. The purpose of this chapter is to help us understand the African concepts and practices around friendship and put ourselves in a position to develop them.

Juma: The question is, how committed are we?

Wesley: The question is, how much do we enjoy each other?

The degree to which we like someone's company does not determine the strength of an African friendship. It's quite possible to enjoy someone without being committed to him or her.

Commitment, the core of African friendships, is commonly demonstrated through actions of solidarity, such as participation in each other's major events (weddings, funerals, key family events), sharing resources (such as money or food), and finding practical ways to be supportive during difficult times.

A Canadian friend reflects, "In my country, there is no expectation of entitlement to help in times of need. Your crisis is your crisis, not my business." On the contrary, committed African friends are willing to take ownership in each other's problems. In fact, one way to ripen a potential friendship is by inviting the other person to get involved when there is a need.

When Westerners are asked for money, we hear it as a request—which it is—but on a deeper level it is also a proposal. It's a proposition. It's a way of saying, "What would you think of us taking this relationship a step deeper?" Gifts are symbols that mean, "Yes, we are together. You can count on me."

The following table breaks down the African categories of friendship as I understand them:

Table 4.1. African categories of friendship

Level of relationship		Level of commitment
Strangers	>	I have no obligation at all (possibly alms among Muslims).
Casual friends and relatives	>	I should help if I can.
Close friends and close relatives	>	I must do my best to help.
Immediate family (parents, children, siblings)	>	All I have is yours.

A friendship may start with two acquaintances and become deeper over time, or a deep relationship may gradually cool. Friendships are dynamic. Over time they may grow deeper or they may gradually cool. Redefinitions of the relationship often occur around times of crisis.

When someone offers help he offers a deeper level of relationship, and when the other party reciprocates this commitment, the deeper level is confirmed. When one party does not respond to a request for help or does not reciprocate help already given, it communicates that he is not ready to deepen the relationship. In this way, friendship and commitment are inseparable. They define each other.

The Cost of Friendship

An obligation is a duty, a responsibility, which is due from one person to another. As an American, I prefer not to feel obligated, or duty-bound, to my friends, because that would detract from the pleasant atmosphere between us. I also don't want my friends to feel like they have debts toward me; if someone owed me a debt, I would want it quickly settled. A North American friend adds in, "For most of us, 'goodness of heart' means that there is not a sense of obligation."

Juma: Close friends have deep obligations to each other.

Wesley: A sense of obligation would be a wedge between friends.

Africans don't see friendship this way. Maintaining a pleasant atmosphere between people is obligatory, but it doesn't mean two people are real friends. If a friend is an ally, he is duty-bound to be helpful. An ally who doesn't do anything isn't worth very much. A friend who does not help in a time of need is not a friend.

This concept of friendship can be a significant barrier in potential Western-African friendships, because we generally don't expect to express our friendship in material ways. For example, we may be very comfortable giving emotional support but instinctively nervous about becoming financially involved in a friend's problem.

"You need to know there's a huge price tag on deep friendship," Achieng advises us Westerners. Achieng, a Luo by ethnicity, is a well-respected woman in her social circles. "Decide in advance how far you're willing to go (not in the middle of a crisis). Are you up for this? If the answer is no, be prepared to have acquaintances."

Although no one can force us to adopt the "friendship as allies" system, our African friends will interpret our behavior through their own lenses. "There is no way in which friendliness can substitute, or be compensation, for failure to meet material obligations," says anthropologist Peter LeVine (as quoted in Maranz 2001:64).

Juma: A request for money is normal between friends.

Wesley: Friends generally don't get involved with each other financially.

Although Westerners may ask their friends for money only as a last resort, exchanges of material goods are ubiquitous in African friendships. In fact, an African friendship that lacks material exchanges barely counts as real friendship at all. This difference in expectation can cause tension in cross-cultural friendships.

To be more specific, Westerners are likely to experience some degree of discomfort or irritation when their African friends ask for money. I know that I feel tense and perhaps a bit defensive when I sense that I am about to be asked for money. In our culture, requests for money between friends are not common and may cause us to feel awkward, or even think that the other person is trying to take advantage of us.

To illustrate the different perspectives on this matter, let me share a story I heard from an American friend, Lin. I took the liberty to recreate the story from the perspective of his African friend, based on accounts I have heard from other African people in similar situations.

Lin and Ouma

A North American named Lin visits his daughter living in Kampala. He is a very outgoing man, making friends with everyone he meets, even an old watchman who works for his daughter's family, Ouma.

Lin's story

"Ouma was such a fascinating man. He has two wives and twelve children! I learned so much about Africa from him. At the end of my visit, I asked him for his postal address so we could stay in touch.

"We exchanged a few letters in the next couple months. Then, six months after I left Uganda, I got a letter from Ouma in which he asked me for money to help pay his daughter's school fees. He said the total was about $300.

"I was shocked and disappointed. I thought Ouma was my friend. But I guess he just used our friendship to try to get money. Besides, I had no idea what to do. Should I pretend I never received the letter? Should I say I can pay the fees once, but he should never ask me again? It was so awkward that I just stopped replying to his letters."

Ouma's story

"One day my employer's father came to visit. He took a great interest in me, inquiring about my family and farm upcountry. I was surprised and honored by his attention to me, a stranger and common farmer.

"When it was time for him to leave, he asked me for my address. Wow, I thought, this man really wants to have a relationship with me. In the following months I wrote him a few letters to see if he would reply, and he replied to each one.

"January school fees for my children were coming due, so I decided to see if Lin was ready to take our relationship to the next step. I told him about our need. I was able to pay part of the bill with the money I earned at my job but told him what the total fee was so he would understand that my daughter goes to a good school. From our other interactions I was confident that he was the kind of friend who would chip in.

"I never heard from him after that. I was really disappointed. Why did he write me those letters if he didn't want to be my friend? It was confusing, so I didn't write to him again."

In this true story, the potentially rich and meaningful connection between Lin and Ouma was truncated by simple misinterpretations of behavior. This might have been different if they hadn't both assumed the other person was operating with the same cultural norms.

Reciprocity for Healthy Relationships

Whenever possible, move relationships to a deeper level by exchanging goods that both parties have the capacity to swap back and forth, such as bananas from your trees or an extra outfit from your closet. By sharing items that can be reciprocated, we build friendships without encouraging dependency.

"People don't become dependent by giving them money or gifts," says a Canadian friend in Burkina Faso. "People become dependent when you demean them by refusing to accept the small gifts they can give back."

To steer a relationship in the direction of a peer-to-peer friendship, I encourage Westerners to give gifts that can be reciprocated. For example, I like to give mangoes from the tree in my yard or a chicken from the small flock of laying hens I keep. If we give gifts that are much larger than the recipient is able to reciprocate in some way, she is more likely to think of the giver as a donor than as a friend. In the case of my mangoes, it is not a hardship for the average African to respond to me with a similar gift.

When the situation is turned around, and *you* are the one receiving a gift, make it a priority to find some way to reciprocate. Don't merely thank the giver. Within a month or two, find a way to give her something of approximately equal value.

Social Networking

Juma: Friendships are often based on a network of family and clan relationships.

Wesley: I can strike up a friendship with anyone.

Africans generally expect to develop friendships with people of the same gender, age group, and people who fit into a similar socio-economic class. Ethnic affiliation plays a role as well, as people are generally more trusting of someone from their own group. Trust and loyalty are seen to start with the family, then radiate outward to the clan, and then to the larger ethnic group.

People of other ethnicities, Westerners as well as other African ethnic groups, are beyond the reach of this implicit trust. Muriuki, a member of the Kikuyu ethnic group, is the mother of a girl in my son's class at school. She acknowledges that her family's rule of thumb was "stick to your own" [ethnic group] in friendships. "Friendship with people from other ethnic groups is only for reasons of business."

> **Juma: Friendships develop slowly over time.**
>
> **Wesley: Friendship starts when I feel a "click" with someone, and can develop fairly quickly.**

Among the many African ethnic groups, each one has its own distinct customs and expectations, which can lead to misunderstandings in cross-ethnic friendships. "It's hard to avoid embarrassment when we don't know what the expectations are," says Wanjiku, a Kenyan woman, "and everything in the African community is about saving face."

The preference for family-based friendships puts Westerners in a tricky position. "When it comes to Westerners," Wanjiku continues, "the degree to which they are unknown and mysterious makes us want to leave them alone. Things are so unclear."

Intentionality and Commitment-Based Friendships

Mutual gifts cement friendship. (Proverb from Cote d'Ivoire)

"Our pace of friendship is much slower than yours," Achieng told me. A real friendship is established slowly, where loyalty and solidarity are tested by time and crisis and proven reliable.

Achieng also mentioned the importance of vetting friends. "I'm sorry to say this, but there is a lot of concern about jealousy and competition." There is a sense that one should "vet" new friends to make sure that they are sincere, not merely opportunists, or even competitors, who feign friendliness in hopes of gaining some personal advantage.

"So what if we laugh together, Debbi?" my friend Muriuki said pointedly. It's easy to enjoy someone's company, to laugh, to chat, to share a coke— these come naturally in good times but don't prove that a friendship is genuine. A "click" in good times proves nothing at all. Simply put, African friendships are neither quick nor cheap.

Juma: We are not quick to express personal thoughts and feelings.

Wesley: We are generally open with our friends about what is on our minds.

The boundaries that differentiate public and intimate information vary from culture to culture, but in many contexts there are topics that friends do not talk about openly. In my culture, for example, personal finances are off limits for discussion. I don't know any details about what my friends earn, and it would be considered invasive to ask questions about it.

In African friendships, there are also topics that are out of bounds, including money, sex, health, and success, according to Achieng. (Talking about your own success might arouse jealousy in your friend.) But the off-limits subject that may surprise us most is personal information: one's personal world is considered a private domain, about which it would be invasive to ask many questions.

In the West, when we meet someone, normal conversation often follows along the lines of *What do you do? Where do you live? Do you have a family?* To us, these types of questions communicate friendliness and benign interest. To an African, however, those questions may feel invasively personal. "I think Westerners have traditions of talking about everything," said one African interviewee. "They have no curtains."

Although Africans are excellent conversationalists, comments about personal thoughts, hopes, plans, and preferences are curiously absent in most conversations and an African friend may find it disconcerting if questioned at length about such things.

It is better to make conversation around public topics, like community events, public opinion, other people, celebrations, the weather and farming, new construction in the area. These topics are communal in nature, instead of individual and private.

"Small talk is an art form in every culture," says an American friend in Mali. "We must learn how to make it." It may feel that these things are superficial, and in a way they are, but your African acquaintance is probably happy to use this neutral conversation to get a better feel for who you are. This kind of small talk is a safe place to learn indirectly about each other without the awkwardness that potentially rides in on premature intimacy. There is a sense that we give a friend permission to "know about" something when we bring it up. "If you've never mentioned it, I can't ask about it" said one African about the protocol in her ethnic group.

Gifts and Other Dues

My advice to Westerners is this: gifts and requests are not random. Take time to think it over; don't just blunder into something. (Achieng[1])

Juma: Gifts may be more than mere generosity.

Wesley: Gifts should be genuine and "from the heart," with no strings attached.

In Western cultures, we tend to think that gifts given "from the heart" (without any strings attached) are the most sincere, and hence the most valuable. This is a trait of societies that emphasize individuals instead of collective groups, says Lederleitner (2010:42). In African and other collectivist societies, however, gifts work differently.

In the African context, although gift-giving between friends is common, gifts are not given randomly. As a type of non-verbal message, gifts often communicate something, and the message may be a very calculated one.

---

[1] Personal communication, April 2, 2014.

According to Achieng, sometimes a gift is given as a test of friendship. The recipient responds to complete the transaction, and the type of response given sends a message. If you respond by reciprocating a gift-in-kind in some way, the friendship deepens. If you don't reciprocate, or reciprocate with a lesser gift, the relationship cools slightly. In this way, exchanges of gifts can "take the temperature" of a relationship.

Without reciprocity, no friendship exists. (Duane Elmer)

Another use of gifts is to create obligations on the part of the other person. Someone may give a gift in anticipation of his own upcoming need, as a way of better positioning himself to receive the other person's generosity. A Westerner from Northern Ireland, working in Mali, told me of a time when one of his American colleagues gave a significant financial gift to his neighbor in the village. The neighbor, interpreting the gift through his African lens, was horrified: "What huge service is the American going to ask me to do for him at some undetermined point in the future?!"

An obligation prompt

An American development worker among the Maasai of Kenya told me this story:

"Several days after I had moved into the village, a man from the community came to my home with a goat. He explained that he was giving it to me as a gift, to welcome me to his village. Of course I accepted his generosity.

"A few days later, he came over again. He asked my wife if he could borrow a cup of sugar. She immediately gave it to him; after all, he was our friend. Several days later, he came by again with another need. And then another, and another.

"I soon realized I was in a predicament. Since he had so generously given us a goat, we were not in a position to refuse any of his requests. That 'friendship' cost me hundreds and hundreds of dollars over the years."

Juma: What is an inconvenience between friends?

Wesley: It is important to avoid inconveniencing one's friends.

African friends expect to do favors for each other. Of course, it can be an inconvenience, but it is a fact of life. In a commitment-based friendship, a little inconvenience is not a big deal.

Wanjiku, a Kenyan woman who is married to a British man, tells this story:

"We went to the UK for a visit, and I wanted to do some shopping to stock up for the next few years in Kenya. I have four young children and didn't want to drag them along to the stores, so I started asking friends and relatives if they would help watch my kids for me.

"People said, 'No!' They said they had other things scheduled. Their plans were a higher priority than I was. Even if it was just that they were visiting a national museum (which would be open all day), if they had planned to leave at 10:00, they would say, 'We can watch your kids until 9:45,'—and they expected me to get my kids at 9:45!

"They did not adjust their plans for me. The message I got was that I was not a priority for them, and that my kids were an inconvenience," concludes Wanjiku.

"You cannot refuse the request of a friend," says another Kenyan woman. "There is a very present sense of give and take: today you need help but tomorrow it is I who will need help so we must work together. It's important to flow with this give-and-take as much as possible because to show stress (instead of graciousness) might communicate that the person is not a priority."

Juma: Friends must have time for each other.

Wesley: Time for my friends depends on my schedule.

In the West we have a tacit understanding that our relationships must fit around the demands of our work. If a friend calls when I am on the way out the door to go to my job, I can politely explain that I can't talk right then, and she probably won't be offended. She would do the same thing to me.

In Africa, it's the opposite—work fits around relationships. People are always more important than schedules and deadlines. If a friend drops by when an African is on his way out the door to work, he must not brush off his visitor. It's normal to stop, go back inside, and serve tea to his guest (or arrange for someone else to fulfill his hosting duties). The guest expects this and would do the same. In Africa, we must never ignore the people around us, no matter how busy we are or the urgency of our work.

In my interviews for this chapter, I consistently heard African voices saying that we Westerners are too speedy—too speedy, in that we try to develop friendships in short amounts of time, and also, that we try to do it without investing a quantity of time. We are always in a rush. Friendships take time, they emphasized, and that time must be relaxed. Among African friends, it is essential that they feel their friends genuinely have time for them.

Juma: Simply being together is the essence of friendship.

Wesley: Our friendships often revolve around activities.

In the Western context, we often do things together with our friends, and there are many things to do: go to movies, restaurants, concerts, or sporting events. Particularly in rural Africa you may find that none of these entertainment options are available. Instead, friendships revolve around doing the simple things of life together.

As I interviewed Africans for this chapter, a repeated theme was their value of being together, rather than doing things together. It's important to be with people where they are, in their normal environment, however it is, as a way of showing acceptance of them and their reality.

Showing solidarity with friends, especially in times of hardship, is extremely important. It doesn't have to be exciting—we just need to be present. An American friend who grew up in Burkina Faso puts it simply: "The obligation is to *sit, not to talk.*"

> *Being together is the essence of friendship.* (Clemence, from Kenya)

Being together

Clemence, a Kenyan interviewee, told me this story:[2]

"The wife of a good friend died, so I went, along with a group of people from our city, to his village to participate in the burial.

---

[2] Personal communication, April 2, 2014.

"The upcountry home was packed with people. I slept in a small bedroom with ten other ladies. Mattresses were squeezed onto the floor, and as the floor didn't have space for ten mattresses, some of the ladies spent the nights in upright chairs. There wasn't enough water for everyone to bathe....We did this for three days.

"For us, these times are about being together. There's nothing more important in friendship than being together. The issue is being together, solidarity. This is much more important than the particulars of what we eat, if we eat, if we have places to sleep, or if there are enough bathrooms."

Collective Friendship

Coming from an individualist culture, Westerners are likely to feel that a friendship with another person begins and ends with the two of us. In the African family, however, individuals almost think of themselves as a collective noun—like bees, for example—whose identity, productivity, and even their very survival is interdependent with one another. Among collectively- minded people, it is impossible to be connected to a person without being, by extension, connected to his family system. To be my friend's ally is to be an ally to her whole family system.

Juma: I have obligations to my friends' families.

Wesley: I do not have any obligations to friends' families.

Most often, this takes the form of helping a friend fulfill his obligations to his family. A person in crisis is entitled to the help of his friends; a person whose family system is in crisis (even if he personally is not) is similarly entitled to help. Asking one's friends for help for a family member is considered normal and acceptable.

The company car

A North American NGO worker in Mali told me of the following incident:[3] "A Malian employee wanted to take his elderly mother to the Christmas service at their church, but he felt that she was too frail to go by public bus. Instead of hiring a private car to take her (which would be the normal solution), he

---

[3] Personal communication, May 20, 2012.

asked me, his supervisor, for permission to take her in one of our organization's private vehicles.

I wasn't sure what to do, because from my American perspective, he should not use the company vehicle since it was not company business. But I was also aware that from an African perspective, his request was legitimate, and I had some level of obligation to help him help his mother."

> **Juma: It is very important to participate in community events.**
>
> **Wesley: Participation is voluntary—and assumes you are a very close friend of the people involved.**

In Africa, participation in events like weddings, funerals, ordinations, parties, etc., is important because it shows solidarity with a family (or a community). By attending your African friend's event, you communicate that you are "for" him, and that he has your support.

Although you may not get a personal, written invitation, these types of events are assumed to be public, in that they are intended for the whole community. When a wedding or funeral takes place in the village, the whole community participates. The event planners do not limit the number of people who participate, partly because African hospitality forbids such limitations, and also because a large gathering indicates that the family involved is well loved.

Practically speaking, there are a number of reasons why foreigners may be hesitant to go to an African event, including the likelihood of an unpredictable schedule, long duration of the event, and the possibility that it will be in a language we don't understand. If the event is a circumcision ceremony or revolves around aspects of traditional African spirituality, we may be particularly eager to avoid it. These considerations are real and deserve attention. However, let's bear in mind that African friends interpret our behavior according to their culture, not ours. "Africans easily interpret the behavior of Westerners as evidence...that they do not care to show solidarity," says Maranz (2001:97).

If you are unable to attend a friend's important event, it is appropriate to send some sort of gift in your stead (money will do) to communicate your goodwill to your friend.

Hospitality

A visit is an honor; everyone hopes to have guests.

African friends are accustomed to visiting each other freely and spontaneously. It is an honor to be visited, and everyone hopes to have guests come to his home. Since guests are a blessing—as the Swahili saying goes: *wageni ni baraka*—hosts usually are happy to adjust their other schedules to cater to a visitor.

Although the protocol of many Western cultures requires that visits be arranged in advance, this is not a component of African hospitality. Typically, African friends would set the date and time of a meeting in advance only if there was something serious and urgent to discuss, "like a dowry, or a serious family conflict," says Muriuki. So, in spite of what we have been taught in our home cultures, Westerners should be careful about pre-arranging casual visits.

Juma: Visits are usually spontaneous.

Wesley: A visit between friends is usually planned in advance.

Cross-cultural expert Duane Elmer (1993:14) says, "In many parts of Africa, an invitation to come to my house at a designated time may not be interpreted as friendly and loving. In fact, it might be interpreted as a sign that I want a formal, distant relationship. Why? In Africa one shows friendship by stopping in unannounced."

We should also be aware that visits may last longer than they normally would in our home countries. In my home context, one and a half to three hours is the "appropriate" length of a visit, with the rare exception of a longer visit if I am visiting my siblings or extremely close friends. In those cases my extended visit would have been planned for weeks. Visits between Africans can last much longer than this.

When the guest is ready to leave, she should approach her departure with a degree of delicacy. A gracious guest usually says something like, "I'm sorry I need to leave so early." Or "I wish I could stay longer." The hosts are expected to protest—at least to feign disappointment—as a way of showing that they appreciated your visit.

A Dutch friend who grew up in Burkina Faso says this: "In Burkina Faso, proper leave-taking etiquette requires a guest to *"demander la route,"* which literally means to request the road, i.e, to request permission to leave. The host has the right to completely ignore your request. As much as an hour or more later, she may say, "Oh, I think I heard you say you were ready to leave," and grant permission. The guest does not unilaterally decide when the visit is finished. It would be totally inappropriate to glance at your wristwatch and stand up."[4]

On a more formal visit, there may be some type of closing remarks, where both parties express appreciation for the other and possibly a prayer of blessing. When unsure of the protocol, a guest can simply match the pace of the host.

> **Juma: Food and/or beverages must be involved in any social encounters.**
>
> **Wesley: Food is a non-issue; you can have it or go without it.**

Whether a host is expecting visitors or not, the African code of hospitality requires, at the very least, these two things: the visitor must be invited in, and the visitor must be served some food or beverage.

If the guest drops by over a meal time, which is not seen as inconsiderate, he can expect to join the family in whatever they are eating. The cook can always add some water to the stew so that everyone gets to eat something, even if no one leaves the table totally full.

Hosts must feed their guests even if they have to run and borrow from their neighbors to do so. Clemence agrees: "If someone fails to offer food, it sends a message that I don't like you, and I hope you don't stay long." To make it easy for myself, I keep simple snacks on hand—a package of scones or biscuits in the pantry, homemade cookies in the freezer, and a few unopened sodas in the back of the cupboard where my children won't find them.

The sharing of food is done without questions. Notice that African friends don't usually ask, "Would you like something to drink?" The question itself is seen as hinting at reluctance to share and puts the guest in an awkward position. So when you are hosting, just share whatever you have on hand. You can trust your African guests to be appreciative of whatever you serve.

---

[4] Personal communication, March 7, 2014.

Western visitors often ask, "What should we do if someone offers us food?" Sometimes the impetus for this question is a matter of hygiene, and other times it is a concern about eating the food of a family who may be quite poor. In either case, the answer is the same: the food simply must be eaten. The food is a symbol of goodwill and hospitality. To refuse a gift of food, for any reason, is deeply insulting to the host.

When I visit African friends, many times I am served a bottle of soda. On my own, I never drink soda; it upsets my stomach. But the African code of hospitality obligates me to drink at least part of the bottle. If my children are with me, I often let them finish my bottle, or if absolutely no one is watching, I have sometimes poured it out onto the grass. Ultimately it is much better manners to leave the bottle mostly full than to outright refuse it.

In case of a more extreme situation, such as if you have a serious food allergy, there are discreet ways to handle an offer of food. If you are with your family or in a group of people, you may be able to share your portion with someone else without the host noticing. Or you might say something like, "Oh, we Westerners have such weak stomachs, but I can take a few bites." The goal here is to receive the host's hospitality without making a scene.

And while we're here, let me offer one other practical note on food and hospitality: if someone invites his friend to a restaurant, he is taking the role of the host, and as such, it is his duty to pay the whole bill. So when we invite Africans to go out with us, we should be prepared to pick up the whole tab.

Visiting

When Africans go visiting, they often carry a small gift for the host. Standard gifts are basic food items, such as bananas, milk, tea, and sugar, which are used every day. (Wanjiku adds, "Westerners like to give flowers. As an African, I feel like those don't help me. We prefer consumables.")

Juma: Hostess gifts are obligatory.

Wesley: Hostess gifts are optional.

Hostess gifts are part of the reason that spontaneous visits work. We can't assume that the host has food to spare, but by bringing a consumable hostess gift along, you spare your host the possible embarrassment of having nothing to offer if her cupboards (and purse) are empty.

When selecting the gift, bear in mind that, as with any gift, it should be the type of thing that your host can one day reciprocate when she visits your home. As the African proverb says, "There can only be true friendship between equals," so keep the relationship as balanced as possible.

Gifts are especially important if that household is having an out-of-the-ordinary event—a funeral, wedding, or the birth of a child. In the time around these events, families are expected to host so many guests that it can be financially ruinous, and therefore guests are obligated to bring something for the host to share.

Juma: We assume that everyone present is included.

Wesley: We do not assume that someone is included just because he is present.[5]

Among African friends, you can join in with whatever is going on in your presence. When you visit friends, if they are eating, you are welcome to eat, too. And if an event is discussed in your presence, consider yourself invited. Sharing is automatic and instinctive. It is seen as rude to discuss something in the presence of a person who is not meant to be included.

To refuse a gift of food, for any reason, is deeply insulting to the host.

The chapati lady

An American professor tells this story about sharing food:

"When I was teaching at the University of Nairobi, a woman would come around to the offices each day at lunch time to sell chapatis. Three of us shared an office at that time—two African professors and I. If I was teaching when the chapati lady came around, my colleagues would purchase an extra chapati for me. If they were teaching when she came, I would purchase one for each of them.

"This was partly a matter of hospitality between the three of us. But it was also very practical. As well-mannered Africans, they knew they could not eat their chapati in front of someone who didn't have one, without sharing it, and we all wanted to eat a full chapati."

---

[5] This idea is taken from Lanier 2000:55.

Community Gatherings

The African community assumes that life is communal and meant to be shared. Joy and hope must be shared as much as grief and pain. It is possible to carry heavy loads when we carry them together.

> **Juma: In times of crisis, we almost always want to be surrounded by friends and family.**

> **Wesley: In times of crisis, we often want privacy.**

When an African friend meets with crisis, the appropriate response is almost always to go to him. (Don't forget to carry a gift.) In the community where I grew up, we were taught that people want privacy when they are grieving a loss, but I have not found this to be the case in Africa. The general expectation is that people in crisis need to see the support of their family and friends, and that support is expressed by showing up, in person.

The lonely mourner

Clemence told me this story about her American daughter-in-law:
"My daughter-in-law's grandmother was visiting her in my country when she passed away unexpectedly. Upon hearing the news, I immediately went to the home where her body was.

"At the house, I was surprised to find only three other people—my daughter-in-law, a nurse, and the house worker. After a while I realized that no one else was coming! My daughter-in-law had not publicized the news of her grandmother's death.

"After a while of sitting there alone, I started calling *my* friends. Although they had never met the woman who died, they came to the house and sat with me. When I'm going through something, I want people around!"

As friends share back and forth, they become a security net for each other.

> **Juma: Friendships are a form of insurance.**

> **Wesley: My insurance policy is my insurance.**

In the West we have so many layers of security that we don't look to our friends and extended family for it. We have personal safety nets, including savings accounts, investment portfolio, and credit options; and beyond that we have government-backed systems and safety nets: banks, a road system, free education (with teachers and texts!), federal health care programs, disability insurance, and unemployment benefits.

We have an illusion of being very independent, while in reality, we are extremely dependent on these systems as the life support for our lifestyle. Recreational friendships are the luxury of those who already have the allies (or allied systems) that they need.

In Africa, these other systems do not exist. The circle of family and friends is all there is. People want to have many friends and work hard to maintain friendship networks because survival itself depends on strong relationships.

To summarize basic differences in hospitality see table 4.2.

Table 4.2. Western versus African visits

Western visits	African visits
Individuals often meet in a public space (coffee shop, park, restaurant).	Visits are usually conducted at one's home.
People agree on visits in advance.	Visits are spontaneous.
Time is often limited.	There is no time limit; visits can go on for hours or even days.
Food or beverages are optional.	Some sort of refreshment is obligatory.
Hostess gifts are optional and may be an "extra" like chocolates, flowers, or wine.	Plan to take a hostess gift, and it should be practical.
The exchange may only include certain people.	Everyone present is included in the hospitality.

Conclusion

Let me close with a suggestion I was given by some veteran expatriates in Kenya: Find an African person who is a genuine peer or as close to a peer as possible—socially, and in terms of economics and academic level—then feed that relationship. Learn from that person; take her perspective seriously; and invest in the connection.

When we are new to a country and eager for friends, we may be likely to get pulled into donor-recipient type relationships. After all, a generous foreigner can be instantly popular, and the sense of social connection indeed feels good. However, any collection of this type of relationship will eventually become both expensive and also probably limited in the meaningful transparency that can only develop between peers.

In reality, we need to keep a sharp eye out for the local people who are going about their work without much initial interest in us, less impressed by a foreign face, but have greater likelihood of sharing a genuine peer relationship.

More than anything else, we need allies of our own who can offer candid feedback about our developing fluency in relating to Africans. Their honesty, whether pleasurable or not, is a true gift in our movement toward cultural competence.

Questions for reflection

1. What did you learn from this chapter or think about for the first time?
2. Which of the African perspectives presented seemed the most different to you from your way of thinking?
3. When have you observed African friends' behaviors that connected with the observations in this chapter?
4. As a Westerner, what cultural mistakes do you think you may be most likely to make?
5. What ideas from this chapter would you like to discuss further with an African friend?

5

Magic, Morality, and Entities in the Air: Navigating Concepts of Spirituality

African spirituality is not something of the past; it is current and real.
(Magesa 2013b:15)

African Spirituality: Current, Real, Distinct

A missionary colleague, new to work in Africa, traveled from our base in Nairobi to rural Tanzania. He spent a week connecting with a cluster of Maasai church partners, visiting in their homes and participating in church services. Upon returning home, he commented that "I wish they could be a little less Maasai, and a little more Christian."

His off-handed comment grabbed my attention. Granted, it was a slip of the tongue, something he didn't mean to say out loud (and certainly did not mean to have published in a book), but it is important for us, as foreigners, to hear. Many of us think similar things without saying them. It's that idea again that, if we are normal, then we must be the norm—that being right is being like us.

Because we use familiar labels to categorize Africans' religious affiliation—Muslim, Christian, Orthodox, etc.—it may be easy to assume we know more about African spirituality than we actually do. My colleague made a classic mistake in assuming that, as a Western Christian himself, he knew about Christianity among the Maasai. In actual fact, he knew a lot about his North American denomination and almost nothing about African spirituality.

Africa's traditional spirituality is the magnetic core beneath religious practice in Africa today, even though it is impacted by the interface with modernity and other major world religions. It is very much alive and active today. "Any appearance that suggests that African spirituality is inactive is superficial," says Professor Laurenti Magesa. "African spirituality is not something of the past; it is current and real" (2013b:15).

African traditional spirituality is increasingly recognized as an important religious system in today's global village. African theologians are lecturing and publishing materials that articulate traditional spirituality. These materials result in increasingly meaningful inter-faith dialogue with other major religious systems. We have much to gain from this cross-pollination.

Each ethnic group has its own distinct practices, including religious stories, names for God, and protocols for rituals. But in spite of the diversity in forms, there is an underlying unity in the understanding and expression of spirituality that leads us to speak of African traditional religion as one entity instead of many (Mbiti 1969:xiii). A deeper understanding of Africa's traditional religion and practice lends itself to our more fully understanding our African friends and the invisible compass that orients them to reality.

Interactions Between Humans and the Divine

In traditional African life, there is no such thing as an atheist (Mbiti 1969:xiii). God is assumed to exist, and the spiritual world is believed to be engaged in human affairs, always watching, always responding to the human community.

> **Juma: God exists, and controls our lives.**
>
> **Wesley: I determine the direction of my own life.**

Africans traditionally have believed that God controls everything, and ultimately nothing happens without His consent. Sometimes this is called "fatalism," which is the belief that humans are powerless to change what God has predestined. In talking with Africans, we may frequently hear comments that allude to this, such as the Arabic phrase *"Insha Allah,"* which means "If Allah wills it." By using this (or a similar phrase), a person is expressing submission to God and acceptance of what God has determined for that situation. It is not man's duty to understand why God chooses to do things, nor should we presumptuously act like God by trying to control or meticulously plan our lives. The appropriate human response to God's sovereignty is humble acceptance.

> **Juma: The physical and the spiritual worlds are mostly overlapping.**
>
> **Wesley: The physical and the spiritual worlds do not overlap very much.**

A key difference between Western and African spirituality is the degree to which we assume the spiritual world overlaps with the material world. In the African perspective, there is no division, or substantially less division, between the material world and the spiritual world. African spirituality assumes that all physical things have a spiritual aspect, and the two cannot be separated. People's names have religious significance. Trees, rocks, and rivers are not merely lifeless, physical objects; they have a spiritual aspect as well. Dances, certain colors, and any type of rite of passage ceremony are laced with spiritual significance and meaning.

Land, likewise, has spiritual significance. For most Westerners, land is a space of dirt and rocks which can be bought, sold, and developed, while for Africans, land is a powerful part of identity. Generations of relatives have been buried in it, mystically tying the current living family to their ancient past. As I listen to African friends talk about their family's traditional land, I get the sense that the land is almost like a member of the family. "To remove Africans by force from their land is an act of such great injustice that no foreigner can fathom it," says John Mbiti (1969:27).

Another example is rhinoceros horns. For most Westerners the rhino is just a baggy, herbivorous ungulate. Its horn is made of keratin, the same kind of protein that makes fingernails and hair. And while no African would deny this physical reality, some people also believe that a rhino's horn has mystical powers—possibly aphrodisiacal power and the power to cure demon possession. This belief in the spiritual aspect of horn is part of the reason rhinos have been hunted nearly to extinction.

Premises of Spirituality

A sense of the sacred is very present among African people, often showing up in ways we may not anticipate. As we relate to our African friends, we can bear in mind that what we see on the surface may be only a small portion of what they perceive to be going on at deeper levels.

Juma: Spiritual entities interact with us constantly.

Wesley: Are there really spiritual beings out there?

Adherents of traditional African religion believe in a layer of entities that exists between living humans and God. (In some ways this is similar to the Christian concepts of saints, angels, and demons). This layer includes nature spirits, angels and demons, and ancestors (or "living dead"). Africans believe these beings interact with living people on a regular basis.

I refer to these ancestors—these "living dead"—as social-spiritual beings because they are both personal and supernatural in nature. When a person dies, although he has changed form, he remains an active participant in the life of his family and community. The term "living dead" is used to describe the circle of relatives and close friends who have physically died but linger in spirit. The living dead hover around the people they have known in their bodily life.

These people/spirits attend to the petty affairs of the family, like arguments and grievances between family members. They convey prayers and sacrifices to God. When they appear (often in dreams), they give guidance concerning family problems and may warn people of future trouble. They also punish people's wrongdoings, through sickness, infertility, or environmental tragedies (such as droughts and floods). They are almost like an invisible civil police force.

Africans do not worship these social-spiritual entities in the same way they worship God, but they regularly ask them for help and are careful to not offend them. You may notice an African friend pouring out a bit of tea or milk on the ground before drinking—this is a libation and is meant to be a gesture of respect toward his ancestors.

Since these social-spiritual beings are always with us, and are more powerful than humans, many Africans have the sense that their lives are managed, or even controlled, by the spirit realm. A great deal of energy goes into maintaining a right relationship with these beings and living in such a way as to ensure their blessing. This is a very real and important aspect of life in the human community.

Juma: Religion is fundamentally communal.

Wesley: Religion is fundamentally personal.

"In the African world view, spirituality is…a way of behaving, or rather, relating," says Laurenti Magesa (2013b:26). Instead of being private, individual matters, morality and religiosity are very connected to the community. The degree to which someone is seen as an upright or moral person depends on how well he complies with the duties and values his community expects. There is no higher entity, such as a holy book or a pope, which defines what is right and wrong from outside the community.

Integrity, then, is about fulfilling one's obligations—not merely in terms of his private, inner life but also in the community, as seen through the eyes of others. One African friend said simply, "We are defined from the outside, not the inside." Pro-social behavior is understood to be the natural marker of a clean and upright heart. After all, says Magesa, "Does a mango tree produce papayas? Good actions are a sign of good intentions" (2013b:42).

For those of us who come from more individualistic cultures or religious systems where our spirituality is a private, inner matter, we may be inclined to underestimate the importance of our reputations in the African community. It matters very much that one manages his affairs in such a way that he is seen in the public eye as a person of integrity.

Juma: Does it work?

Wesley: Is it true?

In the Christian denomination where I grew up, we spent a lot of energy on developing pristine doctrine. It was critical to believe the right thing, and we had serious problems when members of the church held divergent beliefs.

But in traditional African religion, theology has never been the main issue. It's not about theology; it's much more a matter of functionality. What works? In a context where basic survival can be so tenuous, people's concerns tend to be very practical. Spiritual people and practices that affect real, concrete change pass the litmus test. Who has the power to heal my child? Who has the power to neutralize my competitor?

"Life force" is another expression Africans use to describe spiritual power. Life force is the positive energy that helps people thrive. For example, the life force can help us stay healthy when others around us are getting the flu, or it might give us the competitive advantage in business. Generally, it evokes serendipity.

This emphasis on power makes African society quite nimble when it comes to religious affiliation. It is common for people to consult a traditional healer on one day, an evangelical pastor the next day, and maybe a Catholic priest the next. Let them all pray! And if that doesn't work, a person can continue looking for someone else who can get the job done. "Ordinary people do not rate one religion as better than another. What drives traditional religiosity is the simple question: Does it work?" (Adeyemo 2009:17).

> **Juma: Magic (supernatural power) is a common cause of events.**
>
> **Wesley: If magic exists, it is not part of normal life.**

Magic is a prevalent feature in African spirituality. Most Africans assume that powerful people direct the metaphysical world, frequently and effectively. Diviners and traditional healers are a normal part of village life; their work is something of a cottage industry. It is common for people to go to them in times of need (including practicing Christians) and to engage in rituals or wear special items that channel good magic. Traditional healers and diviners are considered assets to their communities because their craft brings life and health.

Magic can be used for good. If I have a problem—let's say I get sick— I might go to a diviner and ask for help. His job is to consult with the social-spiritual entities on my behalf and determine what is causing my sickness. Have I sinned or offended someone in some way? Then the diviner, mediating between me and the spirit world, helps me to set right whatever I have done wrong. When my sickness goes away, the power of the practitioner is validated.

However, magic can also be used for evil. Bad magic, usually referred to as "witchcraft," is suspected to be at work in cases of sickness, death, defeat, unnatural injuries, extreme poverty, and other sorts of calamity. Practitioners of witchcraft are despised by the communities, and if found out, they are often killed.

Although African people may be reticent to talk with foreigners about magic, "very few Africans, no matter how much education they have, don't believe in witchcraft at some level," says Magesa (2013a).

Chance versus Spiritual Causation

Africans generally believe that bad things happen to people for social-spiritual reasons. Nothing happens by chance. Trouble is *caused*. For example, in the Luo language which is spoken around Lake Victoria, there is no way to say, "I have become sick." Rather, it is expressed as, "Someone has made me sick" (Kirwen 1987:45).

> **Juma: We believe calamity and bad luck are caused by someone.**
>
> **Wesley: We believe bad luck is just bad luck.**

Bad experiences are interpreted in spiritual terms. For example, if someone gets fired from her job, it is not seen as a matter of chance or an issue of job performance. She will probably assume that someone else interfered with her work and think about her colleagues to identify who might have cause to be angry with or jealous of her.

A disturbance in the material world is a symptom of something amiss in the invisible world. The disturbance is usually relational in nature—some personal entity is taking action against another personal entity. A woman may become infertile after she displeases or disobeys an ancestor, or a boyfriend may fall out of love with his fiancée after a competitor manipulates the spirit world.

Natural disasters, such as droughts, epidemics, floods, and eclipses, are also understood to have a deeper meaning: they are a message that something is off balance between humans and the spirit world.

Given this spiritual interpretation, disaster can be doubly upsetting: first, there is the problem itself (say, a sick child); but secondly, there are larger questions it gives rise to about who is trying to hurt us and why. In working alongside Africans through trauma or crisis, we should be alert to the social-spiritual concerns that are involved.

Spirituality in the Social Environment

Since problems are understood to have origins in the spiritual world, African communities naturally look for spiritual ways to address them. Traditional healers and diviners can lead in healing/cleansing rituals to resolve people's problems. The purpose of these rituals is to set things right, to mend the social-spiritual disruption so that harmony and balance can resume.

In traditional ceremonies, good spirits can be called upon, and bad spirits can be expelled or neutralized. Sometimes herbal medicines are also used in cases of medical problems, although they are viewed primarily as carriers of spiritual force.

> **Juma: We resolve problems through spiritual means (cleansings, rituals, healers, diviners).**
>
> **Wesley: We resolve problems through scientific means (doctors, medicine, therapy).**

When evil breaks into a family or village, in the form of conflict, sickness, or murder, all the people who are involved must be cleansed in order to neutralize the evil force. If the evil force is left unaddressed, it might continue to wreak havoc in the community. The cleansing also breaks the connection between the people and the evil entity. Evil must not be allowed to linger around a homestead because it gives out something like bad spiritual radiation.

For example, my friend Atieno, a member of the Luo people, told me that her group traditionally handles the dead body of a barren woman differently than the body of a fertile woman. When a barren woman dies, their custom is to discard her remains in the bush without a proper burial. By disposing of the body with ignominy, the family asserts their will to be disconnected from the destructive energies that caused her infertility.

It is important that ceremonies be done in the proper way so as to have the proper effect, even though it may be very expensive. Luo people believe a corpse must be returned to his home plot and be buried with lavish ceremony (even if he is living abroad). Transporting corpses can be a financial nightmare, as is a lavish ceremony. But they believe it to be an essential part of the burial ritual, and if not done properly, the dead person may return in spirit form to his family members. It is in the vested interest of his family to give him a good sendoff, as good a one as they can afford—even more than they can afford—to keep him happy. An unhappy ghost is a real bother.

Last year's cholera outbreak

This story is told by an African elder[1]:

"There was a plague of cholera last year when forty people died in a nearby village, and everyone was afraid it would come here. Do you know how it was warded off? The heads of each household were called together and told to purify themselves of all evil thoughts and feelings and to reconcile themselves with anyone with whom they were at enmity.

"Then, on a designated day, all the heads of the households gathered early in the morning at the river, each bringing dirt swept from the floor of his house. This dirt was then mixed together and thrown into the river by a respected·elder. He prayed that the evil thing would leave our village.

"Not one person died of cholera in the entire village."

---

[1] Kirwen 1987:30

Engaging Spiritual Leaders in the Community

As Westerners working in Africa, I recommend that we intentionally engage spiritual leaders to confront problems in the communities where we work. Because of our more secular worldview and our inclination toward technological, scientific, and medical solutions, we may forget to consider potential spiritual solutions.

Village elders, community leaders, pastors, and imams are usually more in touch with the pulse of a community than foreigners are. It is wise to consult with them about community concerns. A spiritual leader might be able to engage a troubled community with meaningful rituals that resonate deeply with the people. How would we evaluate whom to consult?

Community versus Individual Moral Code

The African moral code orbits around relationships. Wrongdoing is measured by how it impacts the bond between people. Evil is, according to the African definition, anyone or anything that threatens or diminishes the vitality of a community. And the flip side to that is that a behavior which has no impact on harmony between people cannot be considered a serious sin among Africans.

> **Juma: Wrong-doing ("sin") is anything that violates relationships.**
>
> **Wesley: Wrong-doing ("sin") is anything that violates a rule.**

This can be a very tricky one for Westerners to internalize. I was taught that "to sin" is to break rules—don't steal, don't cheat on tests, etc. It is always wrong to break these rules, regardless of whether anyone finds out. This takes us in a rather different direction than does the cultural predisposition of our African friends.

Because of the African definition of morality, Africans may be offended by behaviors that Westerners consider acceptable and accept some behaviors that we consider offensive. Here are a few examples of things that are considered wrong in the African context.

Improper Behavior Among Africans

- Refuse to share what you have
- Insult an older person
- Lose your temper
- Refuse to marry and bear children

Since we see morality through a different lens, these right and wrong behaviors may not be intuitively obvious to us. Because of the gap between our definitions and an Africa's definitions, Westerners in Africa may be tempted to undervalue and pay inadequate attention to the role of smooth and harmonious relationships in the African community.

A late night indiscretion

The following story was told to me by an American who grew up in Burkina Faso. I tell this story here to illustrate how one problematic situation was understood, viewing morality through the African lens:

"A man went to the city to look for paid employment and left his wife and children to work their family farm. He was gone for a long time, and eventually a neighbor man started coming around to visit the wife at night. After their rendezvous, the neighbor would always slip away and spend the night at his own home.

"One night the man fell asleep in the woman's bed and left the house the next morning, after the day had already begun. The village was outraged. Of course, they had known very well that he and the woman were sexual partners, but his discretion in coming and going showed respect for her marriage. The day he left her house after sunrise he dishonored her husband and the general order of the village.

"In the eyes of the community his real sin was not that he dishonored God by sleeping with another man's wife but that his carelessness disrupted the harmony between him and his neighbor and brought embarrassment upon that man."

Wesley: If that is how sin is defined, how do Africans define "good"?

"Good" is anything that builds harmony or strengthens the vital force of a person or group. Behaviors that point to longevity, honor, prosperity, harmony, health, generosity, and fertility are generally considered good.

There are many places where a Western and an African sense of "good" or "upright" overlap. When someone welcomes a visitor into their home and serves them hot tea, for example, their hospitality feels good—it feels right. However, instead of focusing on the aspects of African morality that are intuitive to Westerners, I want to draw out the points where Westerners and Africans see things differently. (We can handle the places of overlap easily enough.)

See some examples, below, of behavior that is considered correct in the African context but may seem strange to Westerners:

Proper Behavior Among Africans

- Overlook a small offence or injustice (promotes harmony)
- Hide or ignore information about a wrong (promotes peace)
- Go along with the group, even if you don't personally agree (solidarity)
- Help a clansman get an opportunity (family loyalty)
- Take several wives and have many children (fertility)
- Go into debt to help a relative (generosity)

These behaviors are seen as being good because they honor the most sacred African values.

No children, no chance

The following classic scenario further illustrates the ancestral values of family and fertility:

An African man marries a young lady, and soon it becomes evident that she is unable to conceive. This is devastating news because it means that her ancestral line of vital force has come to an end. Her husband may send her back to her family, or he may keep her but marry other wives so that his line, at least, can survive. The community views this as acceptable because his duty to his parents and ancestors overrides his duty to that specific woman.

Juma: My community defines what is right.

Wesley: My conscience defines what is right.

In a traditional African village, the community defines expectations and standards of behavior. People are not taught to think for themselves or "follow their conscience." Instead, the leadership of a community decides how to handle situations, and to do right is to comply with their decisions.

But of equal importance is the community's duty to enforce standards. It is the community, both living and living-dead, which traditionally maintains order, usually through some form of social censure.

For example, if a young adult misbehaves, it is his peers who will act as his conscience. Through a variety of techniques, they apply pressure on him, usually quite effectively, to pull him back into compliance with the community expectations. The one who is misbehaving is obligated to cooperate with his peers because his deviant behavior also makes them look bad.

In the absence of a community's corrective measures, deviant behavior is likely to continue because something is only wrong insofar as it hurts the relationships in the community.

Juma: It is wrong to shame others.

Wesley: It is impolite to embarrass others.

To dishonor someone is to make him look bad (poor, weak, ignorant), particularly in front of others. The "sin" of shaming others deserves our special attention because it is taken very seriously in African culture.

Shouting, insulting, and losing one's temper are considered poor taste in the West, but they are unforgivable sins in Africa. If I humiliate another person, particularly in a public setting, I may harm our relationship so profoundly that it can never be fully repaired.

Moreover, the insulted person has an obligation to defend his honor—an obligation that can spin off in all sorts of directions. For example, if one person overtly accuses another of stealing something, the accused is obligated to deny it. And he will deny it, fervently, and may even start a fight about it because the issue at stake is his honor, which is felt to matter a great deal more than the details of what actually happened.

I have heard Western friends express frustration about African colleagues who "lied" to them (which breaks the "Do not lie" rule). But I suspect that in many cases, the African party felt that he was being attacked through a dishonorable confrontation and simply responded in the typical way. Which is worse—to attack someone's integrity or to lie? It seems to depend on where you're from.

Chapter 6 includes a deeper discussion about "saving face" as it pertains to conflict and communication.

The sin that must not be tolerated

The following story is told by an American missionary who worked among the Digo people:

"I was one of three pastors on a pastoral team at a Digo Christian church. At some point, it came to my attention that one of the other pastors was having an affair. Not just a single affair, but he was having sexual encounters with many women from our church.

"I went to this man and confronted him about his behavior. But the affairs continued.

"Next I spoke to the elders of the church. They agreed that this should not be happening, and they spoke to the adulterous pastor. But the affairs continued.

"Disappointed and frustrated, I called a meeting of the congregation. At the meeting, I heard people saying, "This sin must not be tolerated. The person who is doing this should leave the church." As the meeting progressed, I realized that the person the church members were talking about—was me!

"The sin they referred to was *my* "sin." I was shaming the other pastor, shaming the women, and generally disrupting the harmony in the community. My public treatment of an embarrassing situation was much more offensive to them than the other pastor's quiet affairs.

"Ultimately, I had to leave the church because of what I had done."

Juma: Prosperity is the result of good character.

Wesley: Prosperity is the result of discipline, hard work, delayed gratification, and education.

Africans believe that a person's external well-being reflects his internal well-being, that success usually evidences integrity. Those who live in an upright way, in harmony with the living and the living-dead, build up their vital force, that spiritual resiliency, which over time draws down a good life of health and success. "Wealth means God has acknowledged you," says an African friend.

Problems, conversely, are understood to indicate that something is amiss. An evil person cannot prosper in the long run because evil actions are always penalized in some way. Immorality sets in motion evil forces, and a person holding onto evil will ultimately get burned. Or, as my mother used to say: "Be sure your sins will find you out" (Numbers 23:32).

"Be sure your sins will find you out"

An African elder tells this story[2]:

"I remember a former district commissioner who oppressed people by stealing cattle, land, and resources. The people waited patiently, knowing that he would fall on hard times. And sure enough, just a short time after he had retired, the bus on which he was travelling was sideswiped by a truck, and he was split in two by the impact. No one was surprised."

Juma: Negative energy has the power to cause actual harm.
Wesley: "Words will never hurt me."

As a child growing up in the United States, I remember hearing the saying "Sticks and stones may break my bones, but words will never hurt me." Of course I knew that words could hurt my feelings, but it never occurred to me that someone's words might actually injure me physically.

In Africa, however, it is assumed that negative words and attitudes, grudges, jealousy, and hatred all release negative energy. Once released, that energy is set loose in the community. It can cause people to lose their minds, to fall into or out of love, to get sick, or to have bad luck in business. According to Michael Kirwen, this is, essentially, the concept behind African witchcraft—a witch harms others through his/her own negative feelings (Kirwin 2008:51).

[2] Kirwen 1987:47.

You may notice that Africans are hesitant to speak bad news out loud, as in giving a report such as "Her husband is dying." It is thought that, by giving voice to such a situation, the speaker might actually contribute to it, put more energy behind it. This makes the speaker complicit in the bad news he is reporting.

I believe that the pressing commitment to live in harmony with one's community is also connected to this belief about energy. Since unresolved grudges release negative energy, people are highly motivated to resolve conflicts that would otherwise leave them vulnerable to accusation: if you are in conflict with someone and he becomes sick, you will probably be accused of cursing him.

Juma: We believe that ultimately, reality is social-spiritual.

Wesley: We believe that ultimately, reality is material.

In the African view, human existence is primarily a social-spiritual reality with material components, rather than a material world with spiritual components. It is the social-spiritual web that matters most and is most real, more real than the material world.

Although the material world is immediately accessible, it cannot be fully trusted. Spiritual practitioners are able to manipulate things that we see, touch, and emotions we feel, so that what we take in through our senses is vulnerable to interference.

Spiritual entities may have physical landing spots—that is, a certain spirit may dwell in a particular grove of trees, or certain herbs may contain spiritual power. But the physical world is always a servant to the spiritual world. What happens in this life is an echo of what is happening in the social-spiritual realm.

Conclusion

All of reality is spiritual, because it is linked together by spiritual power and is connected to mystery. (Magesa 2013a)

Visitors from the West may be tempted to dismiss African spirituality as strangely dark and superstitious, or simply wrong, as did my North American colleague working among the Maasai (whose story I shared at the beginning of the chapter), but such a view would be quite narrow and pessimistic. Although African spirituality is the twin of neither traditional

Western Christianity nor modern Western secularism, many of its prime values are exceedingly valuable to the global community, including Africa's profound respect for the human community, the earth, and harmony between beings.

Questions for reflection

1. What did you learn from this chapter or think about for the first time?
2. Which of the African perspectives presented seemed the most different to you from your way of thinking?
3. When have you observed African friends' behaviors that connected with the observations in this chapter?
4. As a Westerner, what cultural mistakes do you think you may be most likely to make?
5. What ideas from this chapter would you like to discuss further with an African friend?

Recommended reading on spirituality

African Religions and Philosophy (1969) and *Introduction to African Religion* (1969), by John Mbiti, are classics in the study of African spirituality and religious practice of sub-Saharan Africans. These texts introduce the reader to the primary assumptions of African spirituality, a basic prerequisite for intelligent engagement with African people, both inside and outside religious settings.

African Religion: The Moral Traditions of Abundant Life (1997), by Laurenti Magesa, articulates a traditional African understanding of the most important components of spirituality, including Vital Force, mystical powers and practitioners, and the role of life events in attaining full humanity. This book is important for Westerners because Magesa writes from the place where most Africans exist—inside the uniquely African construct of spirituality, with all of its relevant theological components.

What is not Sacred?: African Spirituality (2013b), also by Laurenti Magesa, describes African traditional spirituality and emphasizes its important contribution to inter-religious dialogue today. Magesa articulates the

African spiritual awareness in a way that makes sense to people from the Western cluster of cultures, even though we generally inhabit a different cultural and theological construct.

6

Riddles and Gifts:
Navigating Concepts of
Communication and Conflict

*A matter dealt with gently is sure to prosper, but a matter dealt with
violently causes vexation.* (African proverb)

Styles of Communication

Where I live in Nairobi, Kenya, English is widely spoken. In fact, in much
of sub-Saharan Africa a foreigner can get around fairly well with English
or French. As a native English speaker myself, it's easy to be lulled into the
notion that communication, then, should be straightforward—after all, we
are all speaking the same language.

However, according to Albert Mehrabian, known for his work on the
relative importance of verbal and nonverbal messages, fifty-five percent of
what we communicate is transmitted through body language, thirty-eight
percent comes from vocal signals, and a mere seven percent of communication is transmitted through the actual words we use (Mulder 2013). These
statistics remind us that there is much more to communication than simply
understanding each other's words.

Literal versus dynamic communication

In cross-cultural contexts, we should also bear in mind that the body language and vocal cues we employ are likely to be specific to our culture and may not be understood by the listener. (For example, avoiding eye contact means different things in different cultures.) If the hearer doesn't catch the meaning, or if he misunderstands it, then the cycle is short circuited. Full communication happens only when the hearer interprets a message in the way the speaker intended.

The widespread use of English makes some things easier for me, like ordering a plate of rice and fish in a restaurant, but it can also lend a false sense of security. In cross-cultural dialogue, people can understand each other's words while completely misunderstanding the meaning. The meaning, of course, is all that really matters. Like a package that comes in the mail, we care about the contents, not the packaging.

In this chapter we're going to look at some classic differences between Western and African styles of communication—differences that hold true regardless of the language we're using. Understanding these differences will help us open the package being delivered, even if it's wrapped in indirect speech and behavior.

One primary difference between African and Western styles of communication is how direct or indirect we are. Compared to Africans, Westerners are usually quite direct: we like to say what we mean, and mean what we say.

Much of the world has a different style, a style in which the way something is communicated matters at least as much, if not more, than what is said. This is a style where, instead of clobbering conflicts head-on, people "come in through the back door," discretely alluding to conflicts through riddles, proverbs, and story-telling.

The following is a short list of differences between direct and indirect communication styles.

Direct and Indirect Messages

Table 6.1 Direct versus indirect communication styles

Direct	Indirect
Openly confront issues or difficulty / Engage in conflict when necessary	Tend to discretely avoid difficult or contentious issues
Express opinions in a frank manner	Express concerns and opinions with tact and diplomacy
Say things clearly, not leaving much open to interpretation	Count on the listener to interpret meaning

Adapted from Peterson 2004:40. Used with permission.

Although there are variations between individuals, as a cultural cluster, Westerners tend to be most fluent in communicating through overt, literal, messages—and to some extent, we may even feel that it's the "right" way to communicate (implying that other ways are inferior). Even so, we don't always communicate directly. Gifts, hugs, silence, and avoidance are other tools we use to communicate which speak without the use of words. During our stay in Africa, we can lean into skills we already have for communicating indirectly and hopefully expand our repetoire.

Information versus Friendliness

Westerners honor each other by being up front, accurate, and efficient with what they say. "We like straight, clear and direct communication," says Duane Elmer, an American expert in cross-cultural dynamics. "We do not like it when someone speaks to us in obscure, oblique, or circuitous ways" (1993:49).

Africans also value honor in communication, but it is packaged differently. In that context, honor is shown through agreeable exchanges. It is seen as "good manners" to keep communication smooth, civil, and pleasant. Having a feel-good atmosphere is so important, in fact, that accuracy sometimes yields the right-of-way to pleasantries. African friends may tell you what they think you want to hear or what will make you feel good—even if the information is, technically, incorrect.

Juma: We generally say the friendly thing, and it may not be intended literally.

Wesley: We generally say, literally, what we mean.

One day I walked to the market and bought more items than I had intended. Unable to carry them home on foot, I called a taxi driver friend to come take me home. "How soon can you get here?" I asked.

"About five minutes," he replied.

As a Westerner, I assumed he meant "five minutes" the way I mean "five minutes," as in, about three hundred seconds; so, after five minutes I went out to stand on the curb. But the taxi didn't come.

After a while I called again. "Sorry, I am delayed," he said. "I will be there in five minutes."

I caught on that what he meant was something more like "I'll get there as soon as I can."

Did the taxi driver lie to me? Not in his mind. He answered me honestly, he just answered a different question: he answered that, yes, he cared about my situation and was doing his best to be helpful.

How to Say "Yes" and "No"

It's not about information, it's about friendliness. (Lanier 2000)

In the West, "no" is simply the opposite of "yes". It is not a bad word or a good word—it's just information. We show respect for other people by giving them information that is factually correct, regardless of how we feel about the information itself.

Juma: "No" and "yes" are statements about our relationship.

Wesley: "No" and "yes" are purely information.

In Africa, "no" almost classifies as a bad word. A direct "no" is too certain, too final, too harsh. It's the way someone might talk to a child; but between adults, it's almost felt to be an insult.

Of course there are times when the answer to a question is not "yes," in which case you find a roundabout way to demur, but preferably without using the word "no." If someone makes a request that you need to decline, it is considered polite to couch your "no" in gentle language.

Respectful Ways to Decline

- I will get to it as soon as I can.
- Maybe another time.
- Let me see if I can do it tomorrow.
- I want to help, but I am not sure I can right now.

Far from being seen as misleading, such replies are seen as courteous. Africans say, "A kind lie is better than a harsh truth." People know their requests cannot always be granted, but they still want to have a respectful exchange. "It's very hard to get an African to say 'no,'" says African interviewee Nakesa who is of Luhya ethnicity. "'No' is rude. And we don't do rude."

Moreover, it is common for Africans to say "yes" when they actually mean "no." Elmer calls this a "relational yes" (1993). The "relational yes" affirms the relationship between the speaker and the hearer. It does not necessarily affirm that the answer to the question is "yes."

Nakesa agrees, "When someone says 'Yes,' you need to figure out which yes she is saying—the yes that means 'no,' 'maybe,' or 'later.'"

A kind lie is better than a violent truth. (African proverb)

African people are more likely to defer to the "relational yes" when there is a status differential between parties. People of lower status would be horribly embarrassed to contradict or to disappoint someone of higher status (Lederleitner 2010:19). As foreigners and guests (which confers a degree of status to the visitor), we are likely to encounter the relational yes. Without realizing it, sometimes we phrase our questions in such a way that our African friends may feel cornered into answering with "yes." We want to learn to word our questions and comments in a way that lend themselves to a factual (as well as polite) response.

Let me give an example. Let's say you are driving to Kisumu town and suspect that you've taken a wrong turn somewhere, so you pull over to ask for directions.

If you say, "Is this the road to Kisumu?" the pedestrian will invariably reply "Yes." By "yes," the pedestrian is communicating something like, "I see that you are on a serious mission and would hate to frustrate you by suggesting that you are going in the wrong direction." Of course this message will not help you reach Kisumu, but at least you have been shown respect.

(The pedestrian will have probably said "yes" with a slight hesitancy in his voice, which is a cue that, although he respects you, there is indeed something wrong with your course. However, a foreigner would have to be very astute to catch the innuendo in his tone.)

You will get to Kisumu much faster if you present the question in such a way that the African man can do what he would do anyway—be polite—and give you accurate information. So when you pull over, you might phrase it this way: "Good morning, sir. How are you? I want to go to Kisumu, but it seems I am lost. Maybe you can help me with directions?"

"I'll be there at 8:00!"

Lisa is an American graduate student I met in Kenya while she was working on a degree in agriculture. This is one of her stories.

"I was assigned a local field assistant to help with my horticulture research. One evening I called him and asked if he would be available to help me do some irrigating in the morning. He suggested we start around 9 a.m.

'It's better to start irrigating earlier,' I replied. 'I want to start at 8 a.m. Can you come then?'

'Yes, okay. I will come.'

"The next morning I arrived at the field plot at 8 a.m. My field assistant was nowhere to be found. At 8:30, I called him on the phone. 'Yes, yes, I am coming,' he assured me. 'I had to take my wife into town this morning to catch a bus to her village. I will be there soon.'

"In retrospect, I realize that he suggested a 9 a.m. start time because he knew he couldn't get to the field before then. When I directly asked him to come at 8:00, he felt obligated to say yes, but that didn't mean he could actually be there at 8:00."

Juma: For accurate information, watch what we do.

Wesley: We try to be accurate in what we say.

Due to the cultural imperative to maintain balance and harmony between people, there are situations in which Africans will not feel free to say what they think or what they plan to do. Nekesa actually went so far as to tell me, "What we say has nothing to do with what we mean."

With this in mind, it is essential that we keep a close eye on people's behavior, which is thought to be a much more reliable indicator of intentions than are someone's words. Of course, a friend says she will help you with a project—she may feel obligated to agree to this—but whether or not she shows up to help will ultimately let you know how committed she is. If she says she will come but fails to do so, there is no need to get angry: she has communicated clearly, albeit not through her words.

In a context where there are limitations to what you can say aloud, directly, we must pay very close attention to subtle messages encoded in tone and body language. Africans communicate a great deal non-verbally, especially in contexts where what is said aloud is somewhat prescribed. We must glean all we can from the quieter cues.

Let's say, for example, that you ask a colleague a question in a meeting. As she answers, you notice that she hesitates, looks away, giggles nervously, or fumbles the flow of the conversation. Something is off. It might be wise not to take what she is overtly saying at face value, at least not yet. Her tone and body language are "saying" what she cannot express out loud: 'There is other relevant information here that I can't verbalize at this time.' You might check in with her privately after the meeting to make sure you heard all she wanted to tell you.

As people who like to be literal in their speech, Westerners listen to what is said and assume that is the entire message. Among Africans, the verbal message is only one part of what is communicated. A verbal message must be understood in light of its context; it may vary significantly depending on who else is around and listening. Don't over-estimate what people say or fail to notice what they actually do.

Managing Conflict

"Do you take dollars?"

One day at a favorite Nairobi restaurant I saw the Western preference for accurate verbal communication butting heads with the African "relational yes." The Westerner heard the "yes" so loudly that she missed all the modifying non-verbal behavior which was, in fact, giving the real answer.

An American tourist was seated in the booth beside mine. When the waiter brought her bill, I overheard her asking if she could pay for it in US dollars. Stammering a bit, the waiter finally said, "Well...yes," but the level of hesitation in his voice was a dead giveaway that something was amiss. Pleased with his verbal answer, the American pulled out a $20 bill which covered the approximate value of her meal. "What exchange rate will you use?" she asked.

The waiter looked confused and then excused himself to go find his supervisor. This was another clue that he did not often receive payments in other currencies.

Next, a senior waiter arrived and said they would take her money, but at an exchange rate that was only 75 percent of the going rate. She demanded to know why the rate was so low, and he explained that it was because she was using such a small bill. So she pulled out a $50. "What rate will you give me for this?"

"Let me confirm." He took the bill and went to the manager.

When he came back, he politely explained that he could not accept that bill because it was too old. (Some Kenyan banks don't accept bills that are more than 10 years old.)

From my perspective in the other booth, it was clear that he was blocking her attempt to pay in dollars. Through the waiters' nonverbal clues (hesitation) and their behavior (making it impossible for her to pay), they were giving the real answer: "No, this restaurant does not take American dollars."

Now they were at an impasse, and neither party knew how to proceed. Understanding the predicament, I spoke up from my table. "Excuse me," I said. "I am an American too. Ma'am, why don't you give me your $20 bill, and I will pay the waiter for your meal in Kenyan shillings."

Relieved, everyone agreed. After she left, the waiters came and thanked me personally for getting them out of such an awkward situation.

Juma: It is rude to blame another person directly.

Wesley: When someone makes a mistake, we should give him feedback.

In the West, we are accustomed to getting and receiving feedback on individual performance. We expect to be informed if we are doing something wrong, and, in the interest of improvement, we assume that at some level, other people want such feedback as well.

In most of the world "this same directness…would be considered rude and immature," says Elmer (1993:48). Directly pointing out another person's mistake is a straight-on attack of the congenial atmosphere we are working to build. It is seen as excessive, aggressive, and directly demeaning.

A more appropriate tactic for handling poor performance is to bring up the problem in a group context. For example, if one of my employees makes a mistake, I might call together the people of that department and say something like, "I want to clarify…." It is important that no one individual is singled out. People who are doing the job correctly will recognize that the message is intended for someone else.

"Don't blame me!"

An American friend who has worked in US embassies in various African countries, told me this story:

"We regularly have to deal with issues of employees arriving late to work. The first step in our protocol is to talk it over with the employee. I usually say something like, "I've noticed you have arrived late several times. What can we do to help you get here on time?"

"With Westerner subordinates, they usually admit that yes, they were late, and commit to do better. End of story. It is quite different with my African subordinates. When I bring up the issue, they usually respond with an explanation, such as 'I was late because of this issue I am having at home with my children.' The idea seems to be that *I* am the one who needs to be more understanding and not make an issue of their tardiness. My friendly chat alone doesn't usually have much of an impact.

"However, the second step in our protocol is to document the conversation. A slip of paper goes into their file, saying that we had a discussion about getting to work on time. To Western staff it's not a big deal; it's not even an official warning. Not so with the African staff. When one of them realizes that documentation has been put in their official file, they get angry.

"It appears to be quite offensive to them, the formal 'write up' for doing something wrong. I have heard the local staff express to each other that 'My manager wronged me.' It's common for them to become noticeably 'cold' toward the person who put the note in their file or to gossip about him/her with other colleagues. The slip seems to mean something to the African staff that it simply doesn't mean to the Western staff."

> **Juma: This makes sense to me. It's an official accusation; it's documented proof that this specific person has failed in some aspect of his or her job. Anyone else who sees the slip will think poorly of the employee. It's just excessive.**

When a Westerner realizes that he has done something wrong, it is often considered a point of honor to take responsibility for his behavior. One way to do this is through an apology. A verbal apology is understood as a gesture of integrity and good will.

> Juma: We prefer symbolic apologies.
>
> Wesley: When we are wrong, we should apologize up front.

Africans do not see it that way. In a culture where preserving one's honor is extremely important, outright verbal apologies are uncommon. It is considered a mark of integrity to handle a conflict in such a way that no one comes out looking bad (including one's self). In general, Africans do not shame themselves by making direct apologies, nor do they expect it from others. Westerners in Africa should be aware that it is almost never appropriate to demand an apology as it may be interpreted as an intentional and excessive move to shame that person.

A Somali friend from Mogadishu explained, "Traditionally our language did not have words for 'please,' 'thank you,' and 'I'm sorry.' We were taught to show it by our actions."[1]

When an African realizes he has done wrong, he may try to set things right in a more indirect way, such as by giving a gift, or offering an extra show of kindness. In the village, when two offended parties want to reconcile, they often slaughter an animal and eat the meat together. This type of symbolic action speaks to their desire for reconciliation, but generally no verbal apology is exchanged.

Verbal apologies

A Kenyan interviewee named Marie tells this story:[2]

"I was at the office one day and made a comment that I probably shouldn't have made about Americans, and one of my colleagues—an American—took offence. He started to argue with me, and, since I realized that my comment was inappropriate, I just dropped the matter.

"For several days after that, he came to my office each day and said something like, 'Look, Marie, I was really offended.' I knew he was looking for an apology.

"I felt bullied." (Notice that Marie made her symbolic move toward peace when she backed off from her comment.) "I didn't feel the need to apologize,

---

[1] Personal communication, November 2013.
[2] Personal communication, May 2014.

and I didn't. Apparently it made him really angry that I didn't apologize, and the situation escalated after that. It got really bad."

Juma: We prefer to approach problems slowly and indirectly.

Wesley: We prefer to attack problems directly and up front.

A conflict situation is a vulnerable time for Africans, a fragile time, when an issue must be addressed without damaging any one person's honor or estranging people from each other. Such a situation calls for discretion and care.

"No one wants to be seen as the person who overtly escalates a conflict," says one African friend. If there is trouble brewing, typically Africans will watch for a long time to see what's going to happen. But they may be hesitant to jump in.

Traditionally African elders have been the ones entrusted with managing situations of conflict. The elders listen to the parties involved, often through private conversations in which an individual can be transparent without the risk of offending.

If someone needs to be confronted, correction can be offered through the medium of storytelling or proverbs. This is a way of 'coming in through the back door,' as one African friend expressed it—that is, indirectly—instead of a blunt confrontation which would surely cause embarrassment.

For example, let's say that an elder from the community shows up at the home of a young couple who are in conflict with their neighbor over a land boundary. They serve him tea, and he enquires about the health of their family and the farm. Conversation is easy and relaxed. Aware that his visit is out of the ordinary, the hosts listen and watch carefully for the message that he is bringing. Near the end of his visit, he recounts an old story about someone else who had a land conflict and how it was resolved. The young couple recognizes that he is correcting them through a message embedded in the story. When they have finished their visit, the elder goes on his way.

Indirect conflict management can take a long time, but it's important that we, as foreigners, are patient with the local process. If we pounce on problems too directly, we can give the impression that we are impatient, or even worse, that we're too arrogant to cooperate with standard protocols. Duane Elmer cautions: "Any sign of impatience or frustration will work against you" (1993:90).

A male goat with sharp horns

The following reflections were written by Don Jacobs, an American missionary to Tanzania and a personal friend of mine, about his work with local church leaders.

"I recall that one time I thought we were getting nowhere as the verbiage expanded; so I asked, 'What is the consensus?' Their answer surprised me, 'Weren't you listening to us?' They had been artfully couching their answers in idioms and stories. They expected me to be smart enough to catch on. 'Oh my,' I thought, 'will I never learn?'

"On another occasion I got frustrated because I wanted a straight answer, and made that known, with vigor. I got my way, but afterward one of the pastors took me aside and gently reprimanded me, 'Today, sir, you were a male goat with sharp horns.' That was not a compliment." (Jacobs 2015:200).

> **Juma: Transparent opinions are only voiced in a safe and private space.**
>
> **Wesley: Transparent opinions can be gathered in public.**

Among Westerners, it may feel normal to discuss an issue as a group, debating and hashing things out, and conclude the matter with a vote. A vote is, for us, a straightforward way to make a desicion.

There are two reasons the Western debate-and-vote approach may not work well among Africans. First, the more sensitive an issue is, the less likely it is to be handled with a transparent public discussion. Usually a leader goes to people privately to hear their opinions and concerns. In many cases, by the time the issue gets to a public meeting, the matter has already been decided informally behind the scenes.

Secondly, Africans traditionally have not relied on voting to make decisions. The people with authority discuss a matter extensively, sometimes coming to a conclusion by consensus. Decisions are often made this way when the people involved are of equal status. Other times, decisions are simply made by the verdict of the primary decision maker. But voting is high-exposure. For one group to win, another group necessarily must lose. Worse yet, if a vote is taken in a public forum, it will be known by everyone exactly who the losers are, which can lead to more bitterness and resentment in the future.

"So what would happen," I asked Nekesa, "if I ask someone for his opinion, and he gives me a false answer?"

This is what she explained: "If you ran into my father and me and asked our opinion on something, I would defer to whatever my father tells you out of respect for him. We are trained to play along. But if my answer seemed strange to you, or was different from what you had expected, you may want to probe. There could be more going on than what is apparent. But probe later, when I am alone, or in a different way, so that I don't have to disagree with my father in his presence."

It is important for Westerners to be mindful of how and to whom we ask questions. The wording and timing of questions can significantly impact the response given.

The Strategic Question

- Is there anything this person stands to gain if he answers in a certain way?
- Is there some way that the answer might compromise his reputation or something else he wants (e.g., a promotion)?
- Is there some way that an honest answer might reflect negatively on friends or relatives?
- Who will overhear his answer?
- How contentious is this issue in his social circles?

Juma: Conflicts are often settled through the use of a third party.
Wesley: We usually prefer to settle a conflict one-on-one.

Growing up in the United States, I was taught to resolve a conflict directly with the other party rather than drawing in additional people. In our culture, this sort of behavior is often interpreted as a lack of willingness to deal with the issue or as a fear of confrontation (Elmer 1993:52).

In the African context, selectively drawing a third party into a conflict is interpreted as a gesture of honor for the relationship. It is a common and effective strategy for resolving conflicts in an indirect way in order to protect the relationship.

Through shuttle negotiation, the mediator helps ensure that the conflict does not get out of control, that no one gets embarrassed or is made to look foolish, that relationships stay stable. "The key is to have a mediator who is trusted by both sides and who can maintain confidentiality," says Lederleitner (2010:152).

Let's say, for example, that Juma is offended by something Wesley does. Juma may mention the situation to a third friend and say something like this: "I don't know why Wesley did such-and-such. I don't want to make a big deal over it, but his behavior seemed so inappropriate. Maybe I'm just not understanding his perspective."

Now of course African people gossip just as much as other people, but there are also culturally appropriate, pro-social ways for two friends to talk about a conflict with a third friend. This can be a sort of coded behavior which the African friend is expected to recognize as meaning something like "There is a problem between my friend and me. As someone who cares about our relationship, can you help us?" The third party decides then if he is willing to help. Using his own discretion about where and how, he will bring up the matter to Wesley in a gentle and non-confrontational manner. Hopefully, Wesley will pick up on what is happening—that someone is trying to help him sort out his riff with Juma. The things Wesley says to the mutual friend about Juma will probably make their way back to Juma at some point. Alternatively, Wesley could respond by initiating a conversation with Juma himself; but either way, it would be common for the conflict to be resolved without ever being overtly acknowledged.

> **Juma: We are obligated to avoid defacing others (and ourselves).**

> **Wesley: We have an obligation to be honest about our limitations.**

I taught sociology for a few years at a university in Nairobi. One day in the classroom a student asked me a question in class that I didn't know the answer to, and I said something like, "I don't know, but let me try to do some research before our next class."

My African students saw this as a strange response. In their context, they explained, teachers would not usually overtly say that they did not know an answer to a question, as that might make them appear ignorant in front of the class. Instead, they would find some way to get around the question, sideline it, or possibly even make up an answer so that their lack of expertise was not exposed. "In general, people will say anything to cover up the fact that they don't know the answer to your question," says Maranz. "People would rather 'lie' than incriminate themselves publically" (2001:190).

"I have found this to be true with the African people I work with," says Anne, an American in Nairobi, who is working on a renewable energy project. "Sometimes the people who run field experiments for our organization can't complete an experiment according to protocol for one reason or another—say the electricity is off that day at the warehouse, which messes up our temperature controls. They still often mark the experiment form as "completed," which compromises our data collection.

"I think they are trying to avoid a situation where it looks like they aren't doing their jobs, even though the electricity issue is clearly no fault of their own. I find it is helpful to specify, repeatedly, that if an experiment cannot be completed according to the protocol, staff should simply write "incomplete" rather than report false inputs. After this was clarified, they were happy to comply."

Westerners may interpret this type of behavior as deceitful. And it is, but let me suggest that in the African context, the issue of honor and shame is seen to be more significant in situations like these than the degree to which a statement is true or false. Although Africans value honesty, when it appears that someone might be publically embarrassed by hard, cold facts, the truth is often softened or avoided for the sake of not making him look bad.

It is exceedingly important to refrain from shaming others, or yourself. Did the waitress botch your order? Is a colleague behind on a project? Don't humiliate someone else. Embarrassing others will only make you look petty and uncouth.

Juma: Conflicts are best resolved through social-spiritual means.

Wesley: Conflicts are often resolved through legal means.

When a conflict arises in the West, it is often settled in court. We generally believe that conflicts are best resolved through a fair interpretation of the terms of contract or relevant law, and not through personal feelings or other subjective considerations (Maranz 2001:116). In this way, our justice system is intended to be impersonal, impartial, and systematic.

From an African perspective, this pre-packaged justice is inadequate. Punishment (or a fine) for a crime is not enough—punishment alone does not heal; it does not restore. Professor Magesa explains that a conflict is seen to be resolved only when the relationship between the two parties is mended, and mended to the extent, ideally, that there is no longer even a grudge between them. When parties in conflict arrive at this point, they often eat a meal together as a symbol that their relationship has been put right again, socially and spiritually (Magessa 2013a).

Traditionally, conflict has been resolved in Africa on a case-by-case basis, personally, and often through the use of rituals. The elders who are presiding over the resolution process consider the individuals and families involved and determine what the defendant needs to do.

Although fines of livestock have been common in traditional village justice proceedings, the ultimate goal is not that a guilty person be punished, but, more holistically, that the wrong be set right in order to re-establish a smooth flow of harmony for the whole community.

Cows, clothes, and criminals

American development worker Clair Good tells this story from the Maasai community where he lived for several years:

"I once knew a Maasai man who, in a fit of anger one day killed his neighbor. He was chased out of his community for this, but after ten years he decided to return and resolve the situation. The first step was for the elderly men from his family to have a parley with the elders from the family of the man he had killed, in which they offered forty head of cattle as restitution for the crime. His elders reported back to him that the dead man's family demanded seventy cows, and he agreed to pay it.

"After the animals had been transferred to the other community, the next step was for the criminal to take his whole family and all of his other livestock to the river. The women, children, and livestock passed through the water to the other side, and then the man himself took off his clothes, washed in the river and put on fresh clothing when he arrived at the other side. This ritual was a symbol of cleansing; the man and all he possessed had to be rinsed from the effects of his crime.

"The third and final step, after the passage of a certain amount of time, was for the man to go to the home of the victim's family and eat with them. In that ceremony, he fed a piece of meat to the leader of the victim's extended family, similar to the way that an American bride and groom may put a piece of cake in the other's mouth at a wedding, and the victim's representative similarly served him a piece of meat. This part of the ritual alluded to the re-establishment of trust between the extended families. After these ceremonies were complete, the man was never again seen as a criminal in the eyes of the community."

Juma: We prefer to make plans face-to-face.

Wesley: We can make plans equally face-to-face, by phone, or email.

Although many Africans have access to phones and email, there is a sense that important matters are discussed face-to-face, particularly if the issue at hand is delicate or complicated.

There are two implications of this preference for foreigners to be aware of. First, the time implications of face-to-face meetings: we can build time into our schedules for meetings rather than assuming that African colleagues would send an email.

Secondly, we can give adequate weight to the African priority of "saving face." Personal interactions must be amicable and polite. A pleasant atmosphere is top priority. Even if a discussion involves difficult subjects, all parties should be able to leave with their dignity intact. This sense of dignity is usually seen as more important than transparency and definitely more important than efficiency.

Personal meetings flow most smoothly when we have adequate time and when we are able to create a safe atmosphere that allows for people to actually express what is on their minds.

Conclusion

Kenyan interviewee Marie works for an international office that employs Westerners and local professionals. I asked her "What is it like to work with us?"

She said, "When our [multi-ethnic] team sits down to discuss a problem, the Westerners tend to 'jump in the deep end.'" (They talk fast and loud, asking questions, shooting out solutions.) "We Africans prefer to wade in to the shallow end." By this she meant that her African colleagues take more time to get to know a situation, learning the players, the interpersonal dynamics, the history, and the hierarchies, before they start voicing their thoughts and suggestions.

Regardless of your nationality, and whether you prefer the deep end or the shallow end, we can add the ideas from this chapter to what we already know about communication. We weren't born as Western-style communication babies. We learned to communicate the way we do, and we can learn more about accurately transferring ideas between people. Communication and conflict will always come wrapped in cultural wrapping paper, but we can move past the way they are delivered; all that matters is what's inside.

Questions for reflection

1. What did you learn from this chapter or think about for the first time?
2. Which of the African perspectives presented seemed the most different to you from your way of thinking?
3. When have you observed African friends' behaviors that connected with the observations in this chapter?
4. As a Westerner, what cultural mistakes do you think you may be most likely to make?
5. What ideas from this chapter would you like to discuss further with an African friend?

Recommended reading on cross-cultural communication and conflict

Cross-Cultural Conflict: Building Relationships for Effective Ministry by Duane Elmer (1993) is an excellent handbook for cross-culture workers (not only people in ministry). Moving beyond good intentions, Elmer helps readers understand and navigate conflict appropriately, whether working abroad or with immigrant populations at home.

Cross-Cultural Partnerships: Navigating the Complexities of Money and Mission, by Mary T. Lederleitner (2010) has a section on common points of conflict in international partnerships. Gracious and concerned for the dignity of all involved, she offers insights for working through these challenges in a way that maximizes the potential of a cross-cultural partnership.

7

Standards, Status, and Resources:
Navigating Concepts of Leadership

Show your superiority by providing for others. (Ugandan proverb)

From Peace Corps volunteers in shaggy clothes and flip-flops to the foreign ambassadors in tailored suits, foreigners in Africa are generally perceived as people of status. While there is no need to overrate ourselves, it is wise to neither ignore nor deny the level of status that local people ascribe to foreigners. Lederleitner confirms this, saying, "Often simply coming as a foreigner with funding will cause others to view you as a person of high status" (2010:51).

This chapter is important for Westerners in Africa, for those of us who occupy official positions of leadership as much as for those of us who don't, because our behavior will be interpreted through the lens of African culture and local expectations. As we develop an understanding of Africa's concept of mature and responsible leadership, we are better positioned to interact with these expectations in a manner marked by competence and graciousness.

The Role of the "Big Man"

*The attitude is, you treat family, friends, and your in-group members the
best you can, and you let the rest of the world take care of itself.*
(Storti 1999:38)

Compared to Western concepts of leadership, I would describe African
leadership as being more parental: African leaders often operate in a
manner that reminds me of the way parents operate in a household system.

Like in a family, there is an unequal distribution of power between "parents" and "children." African culture tends to assume that power will be
concentrated with a few key decision makers "at the top" and not distrib-
uted in an egalitarian way, particularly not between mixed socioeconomic
strata of society. This power distance is seen as normal and appropriate. An
ideal leader may be thought of as a "benevolent autocrat," rather than—in
the more Western way—as a resourceful and respected democrat (Hofstede,
Hofstede, and Minkov 2010:72, 74).

A second parental aspect of African leadership is holism: African leaders
are expected to be personally connected with their "children." In my home,
my children have great access to me as their mother, with only a very porous
boundary between us, in terms of what is "mine" and what is "theirs," and
when and how I am available to them. In our home, my children naturally
come to me, their mother, when they need help or have a problem. They are
always entitled to my protection, care, and advocacy.

Likewise in the African context, there is a porous boundary between a
leader and the people he leads. There is an expectation that he will be sym-
pathetic and responsive to their needs and that he may become personally
involved in their problems. There is not a strict division between his professional and personal duties toward them.

In terms of power and the authority to make decisions unilaterally, African
leaders may have much more social distance from their subordinates than
Westerners are accustomed to, but this power distance is intended to be
balanced by the obligation that a person of status has to be humanizing and
compassionate in relationships with others.

There is much variety in the way African leaders operate; concepts of
leadership differ greatly between ethnic groups and are further influenced
by adaptation to urban realities. One Western friend comments, "I have
found some African leaders to be more intrusive and top-down than anyone

I encountered when a soldier in the US Navy, and some are more laid back and consultative than leaders I interacted with in Australia." As is true in our home countries, we have to know our leaders with some degree of personal closeness in order to know how to anticipate their behavior, and the same is true among leaders in our host cultures. This chapter offers a head start on some of the common differences between the African and Western concepts of leadership.

Juma: Our leaders are highly honored.

Wesley: Our leaders are people, like the rest of us.

Power distance is a well-studied dimension of culture that is closely joined to leadership. Power distance can be described simply as the amount of space between a leader and his subordinates. In Hofstede, Hofstede, and Minkov's research on national cultures, they found that Western countries generally have low levels of power distance, but in African countries the degree of power distance is generally quite high although there is significant diversity from one country to another (Hofstede 2004-2017a).

The table below defines some common characteristics of low- and high-power distance cultures.

Table 7.1. Low- versus high-power distance cultures

Low-power distance	High-power distance
People find it easy to approach and contradict their bosses.	People tend to be afraid of their bosses.
Differences in status between people is minimized.	People accept that power is not shared.
People can speak to each other directly, even about contentious issues.	There are often specific protocols for presenting sensitive issues to those in power.
It is appropriate for lower-status people to ask questions and express their views.	Subordinates should not challenge the opinions of people in power.

Treat men and women in basically the same way.	Expect men and women to behave differently and to be treated differently. People in power are expected to care for those under them.

Juma: A leader's highest responsibility is to relationships.

Wesley: A leader's highest responsibility is to manage a mandate or deliver a product.

For African leaders, duty to their social circles is very compelling. In fact, the duty to use one's position to draw down resources for his community often takes precedence over the duty to an organizational mandate.

Because relationships are always more important than things, like sales targets and organizational objectives, it is considered a sign of moral health and maturity to make decisions that give greater weight to relationships than to financial gain. "Our definition of success is people-centered," says a Ugandan friend.

We can see this principle at work by observing how management handles low-performing employees. Employees in African businesses are rarely fired, even if their work is sub-standard. Firing someone would injure the leader's relationship with that person, which is something to avidly avoid, even when that means that the business may not operate as efficiently as it could. Relationships—not performance—determine decisions.

Juma: Leaders should benefit their own people as much as possible.

Wesley: Leaders should at least try to treat insiders and outsiders equally.

Nepotism is the practice of showing favoritism to relatives, especially in hiring individuals or appointing them to desirable positions (Maranz 2001:114). In the West, nepotism is considered a misuse of one's position; in Africa, however, giving favor to relatives (and friends) is a common, commendable habit.

In the African context, where one's primary allegiance is to the immediate family and clan, people are expected to give advantage to people of their own in-group (usually ethnic group) whenever they have an opportunity to do so. People have a sense that life is unpredictable and unfair, that it's only by sticking together and taking care of each other that a group can survive. Other people's family groups are responsible for them; we will look out for each other.

One Western missionary observed that in her Tanzanian host community, the main consideration in giving leadership positions was "either the relationships between persons, or what could be attained by giving a position to a specific person."[1] Giving a relative an advantage in career, education, or some other form of advancement, is interpreted as a sign of solidarity with him. The leader who leverages his position to benefit his group is usually viewed as responsible and generous.

Implications of Status

Status and position are very important in Africa. In any given encounter, status considerations play a significant role in how two parties speak and behave with each other.

According to Duane Elmer (2002:160–169), the basic building blocks of status are these:

---

[1] Personal communication, April 2012.

Status

- Age: maturity has higher status than youth
- Wealth: success deserves respect
- Rank and position: titles deserve respect
- Education

Specific to the African context, I would add the following:

- Gender: men have higher status than women
- Connectedness: socially-involved persons have higher status than isolated persons
- Guests: visitors deserve honor

Africans prefer to build relationships with people of equal (or higher) status. A person's status increases if he manages to connect with high-status people, but his status decreases if he socializes too much with low-status people. It is rude and inconsiderate to require someone to do business with a person of lower status. When you meet someone new, I suggest that you briefly scan the variables—how many status points do you have compared to the other person? If he has more points, your behavior should show additional respect and deference.

Juma: Status is figured into every social interaction.

Wesley: We are only sometimes aware of status.

Westerners can have trouble respecting Africans' status sensibilities. We aren't used to paying such close attention to status. We have at least a pretense of equality; we want to act like status isn't important. We also may not agree with the determiners of status, particularly the status difference between women and men. Even so, "to ignore [status issues] is to discredit yourself and jeopardize your purpose in being there," says Elmer (2002:151).

To show respect to people in higher social brackets, the important things to remember are, first, that your African friends are probably more aware of status than you are, and secondly, that it's important to pay attention to the small ways that Africans adjust their behavior around people of status.[2] Lederleitner gives this advice:

> If a partner is a high-status person in his culture...it is best if a liaison be assigned to the partnership who is at least of equal status. Then reporting is from one person of status to another. However, some agencies do not exercise care in this area. (2010:50)

Sadly sidelined

I moved to Africa in my late twenties to take a position for which I was well qualified. I did not consider that some of my agency's African partners might feel uncomfortable working with me. But it quickly became obvious that something was wrong. They sidelined me and made it clear in other ways that they didn't want to work with me.

As I came to understand the role of status in Africa, I realized that they felt it was a "demotion" to work with me. I was not their peer. I belonged to a social bracket several notches down from them—because I am a woman and also because I was much younger than they. I had to readjust my understanding of which doors were open to me and which were closed, considering who I am in relation to them.

> **Juma: We show respect through formality and composure.**
> **Wesley: We value collegiality.**

When interacting with someone who is in a higher social bracket than you, it is appropriate to honor that person by using formal behavior.

---

[2] Mary Lederleitner (2010) gives an excellent in-depth and nuanced treatment to working with status issues in cross-cultural partnerships.

Appropriate Formality

- Use a formal register of speech—articulate well, avoid slang and jargon, and use complete sentences
- Maintain composure—sit/stand still, with good posture, and controlled gestures
- Use appropriate clothing for the occasion (probably not a T-shirt)
- Use the appropriate titles for people involved

When a person demonstrates appropriate formality, he communicates that he is self-controlled, mature, and a credible person.

Westerners can identify with these formalities, because we would demonstrate similar composure if, say, we were having dinner with a high-ranking politician. The difference is that in the African context, common people—including grandparents, pastors, guests, and village elders—are treated with this formality. Any person of higher status deserves formality and respect.

You may also notice that Africans, respecting your status as a guest, treat you with formality. Although Westerners sometimes demonstrate interest by engaging a new person in conversation, Africans may demonstrate respect by maintaining some distance: they don't want to act presumptuously by treating you as a peer. Although this can complicate the establishment of friendships, we should appreciate this behavior for what it's meant to show: respect.

Juma: A leader takes ownership for his people.

Wesley: Individuals are responsible for themselves.

I admit that the prescribed behavior in formal African settings exhausts me. The context I grew up in was mostly casual, most of the time. Even for other Westerners who are more dexterous with formal interactions, the cross-cultural aspect will make formalites more tiring than they would feel at home.

When African young people want to relax, often they go to a place that is physically removed from people of higher status so they can "stand at ease." I recommend that foreign visitors do the same. In the privacy of a hotel room or the anonymity of a city café, we can relax, less inhibited, yet without causing ourselves to lose face.

"At home, everyone takes responsibility for himself," says one of my American colleagues in Tanzania. "We assume that, if you have trouble, it's your own problem."

An African leader, in the role of "parent," takes some ownership in the troubles of his subordinates. It's not "every man for himself," as our English saying goes. Subordinates come under the umbrella of their leader's protection and are entitled to any advocacy and help he can provide.

Because a leader is a gatekeeper for his community, his broad personal networks are an asset to the people behind him. If he is well connected, especially to powerful people, it will mean wider access to jobs, political power, education, and other benefits for his community. In a context where everything happens through relational channels strong connections have a real and practical advantage.

This "umbrella coverage" is not necessarily free. To accept a leader's coverage is to accept his authority. Compared to the Western system, African leaders have more vested interest in their people's lives and also much more authority to direct their behavior.

This possibility of being covered by a leader is something we Westerners can appreciate, even though we are used to the "every man for himself" approach. We are particularly vulnerable as foreigners; it is to our great advantage for a local person to take ownership for us.

If you are working under an African leader, you can esteem his leadership by consulting with him regularly. Consult with him on your decisions. Keep him informed of your comings and goings. Although it takes extra time to cultivate such relationships, life in Africa goes more smoothly when you have an umbrella over your head.

A hard-to-get work permit

During a certain political situation in Kenya, the immigration office started denying requests to renew the work permits of Western workers. After years of working in Kenya, some expats were suddenly forced to drop their work and go back to their countries of origin. My organization also had a young couple who was denied renewal, and given two weeks to leave the country.

I explained the situation to an African man who was a father figure to me. He knew someone who worked at immigration and immediately called the man to explain the situation. Several days later, the couple's permit got renewed, and they were allowed to stay.

Juma: A leader uses his own resources to help his people.

Wesley: A leader's personal resources are assumed to be personal.

As the parents of the community or organization, leaders are expected to use whatever resources they have to build up their "household," including their own personal wealth. In the African context, it is legitimate (and normal) to ask one's leader to help—from his own wallet—for a variety of needs.

A leader's ability to help and his willingness to do so, is evidence that he is qualified for his position of authority. (People of lower status are not obligated to share as widely.) The more he contributes to the community, the more connected he is to the people, and as we discussed at the beginning of this chapter, connectedness is a fundamental qualification of leadership.

Westerners expect that people will meet their own needs, independently. As it is not typical to ask one's employer or supervisor for help with personal expenses, Western leaders in Africa may be surprised by how often they are asked to help their subordinates through personal donations. These requests should be carefully considered. "Being a leader in Africa is very costly," says one Kenyan bishop. "You are the resource for your people, and they expect you to give."

Juma: Subordinates expect to be told what to do.

Wesley: Subordinates expect to be consulted.

Western culture values and rewards critical thought and innovation. One African wrote, "Every time I come to the United States, I like to spend a couple hours in a Walmart. I find solutions to problems I never thought of!" (Muriu 2007).

Western leaders in Africa often expect that their local staff will be equally enthusiastic about critical thought and solving problems and can be frustrated to find that innovation and critical thought are not universal values.

In the more autocratic style of African leadership, leaders usually expect subordinates to simply obey. Compliance is the duty of subordinates, not problem solving, not creative thinking. The leader provides solutions; the workers carry out orders.

In cultures with high-power distance, subordinates may be hesitant to even ask questions for fear of trespassing on the space of their leader's position. It is almost never appropriate to analyze or criticize a leader's decision openly.

As Westerners in Africa, it is reasonable to expect the average person to be less enthusiastic than we are about problem-solving. When working under African leadership, we may also need to scale back our inclinations to critique directives from the boss.

Ownership, Control, and Authority

Juma: Leaders serve as general consultants for their communities.

Wesley: Consultants are usually specialized.

In the traditional system, leaders are expected to have the skills to settle disputes and solve problems. Village elders serve as general consultants for their communities and are the authorities on everything: ethics and morality, social issues, politics, economic concerns. They resolve disputes between people and adjudicate the community's justice system. Leaders, too, can expect to be asked for advice on a broad range of topics.

Individuals are not expected to solve their problems in isolation. Given the emphasis on community (instead of individualism), one person's problem is seen as a community problem. As such, it is normal and right to ask for input from wise members of the community.

> **Juma: Initiative means you take ownership for something.**
>
> **Wesley: Initiative just means you want to participate.**

An American college student volunteered to teach art at an orphanage school in Africa. Since the school was quite understaffed, the students expected that the school's administration would be eager to facilitate her work. She was shocked when the school asked her, a volunteering college student, to provide all the supplies needed for the class room and the students.

When a person introduces an initiative, she is expected to support it. As the saying goes, *"Put your money where your mouth is."* Any show of initiative can be interpreted, symbolically, as a statement of commitment and taking ownership.

Westerners, as innovative problem solvers, like to make suggestions. "Why don't we try such-and-such...?" In our context, it is considered good to offer ideas, even if we offer nothing else. But in the African context, an idea is meaningless without real, practical support.

In a context where there are many needs, and leaders are called upon to resource many solutions, African leaders can be guarded about their involvement. They know that initiatives they promote will be dependent upon their personal involvement and their wallet.

The women's conference

A certain church which was part of a larger denominational network decided to host a women's conference. The day before the conference, a group of women got stranded when their bus broke down between their hometown and the site of the conference about ten hours away.

The bishop in the destination town—the host bishop—called the bishop of the town near to where the women were stranded. But that bishop made an excuse as to why he could not get involved with the situation and promptly turned off his mobile phone. Next the host bishop made a call to the bishop in the women's home town, but he also had some excuse and turned off his phone. The women sat by the roadside for six hours.

> **Juma: Of course! The two bishops are making it clear that they are not taking responsibility for this crisis. Whoever takes responsibility here is going to have to pay for a new bus to take them to the conference.**

Finally the host bishop was able to wire money for the women's bus fare to the bishop in the town near them. When he received the money, the local bishop immediately made arrangements for another bus to get the women from the roadside and take them to their conference.

> **Juma: A personal position has the final authority.**
>
> **Wesley: Rules are the final authority.**

Western culture is organized around codified law. We believe in the rule of law; we understand our system of rules to be a "friend" that provides for communal good.[3]

In the African context, rules do not organize society—relationships do. Rules may bend and submit to people in positions of authority. Therefore, the importance of relationships supersedes the importance of rules.

In Africa, impersonal rules are viewed as an "enemy." Formal policies, when written, are often worded in such an ambiguous way that they can be interpreted, by whoever happens to be in leadership, and with great inconsistency, so as to benefit people in power, often by taking advantage of those without power.

Traffic speed is a classic example of an "enemy" rule. Where I live in Nairobi, there are rarely any posted speed limits. However, the policemen (without radar guns) still pull people over and fine them for speeding. When accused of speeding, there is no way to prove one's innocence, even if the driver was carefully monitoring his speed. Civilians assume that the speed limits are just a method for police to take bribe money, not a legitimate way of keeping the roads safe.

---

[3] The content of this section is adapted from Shaw 2012.

Of course not all rules are made to be slippery; many policies are legitimate and functional. But in Africa, much more often than in my home country, there is an expectation that the obstacles that rules create can be neutralized by a person of status who is willing to be an advocate.

How late is too late?

This is one of my experiences with African authorities and rules:

I taught a sociology course for a university in Nairobi one year, and my course finished in April. As usual, there were several students who asked for extensions on their final paper, and we worked that out. But there was one student, Daniel, who did not communicate anything about an extension and simply failed to turn in his paper. My grades were due to the Academic Dean, so I marked Daniel's grade appropriately and submitted the class report.

Ten months later, the dean called me on the phone. "Daniel has submitted his final paper for your class to me, and I want you to mark it."

As an American, I was shocked at this breach in policy. If Daniel had tried to turn in his paper directly to me, I never would have accepted it. But since he had gotten an exemption from the Academic Dean, I had no choice but to grade his paper and give him a passing grade for my class.

This is not to suggest that Western leaders should ignore the formal policies of their institutions but to raise our awareness of the African expectation that rules can be negotiated, and with any luck, trumped. We can be aware that formal policies are sometimes perceived as "enemies" and breakers-of-relationship by our African friends. When we say things like, "our policy does not allow for that," Africans may interpret that to mean, "I don't care enough to help you get around this obstacle."

> **Juma: Our leaders are not fully subject to the rules of the community.**
>
> **Wesley: Leaders are subject to the same laws as everyone else.**

As "parents" of a community, leaders are perceived as the source of order. They define what is acceptable. Since leaders define the boundary between what is acceptable and what is punishable (rather than an external code of conduct), the lines can at times be adjusted to fit their needs. This is sometimes called "impunity," which means the exemption from punishment for unlawful behavior, and it is, at times, assumed to be a *de facto* benefit of African leadership.

In the unwritten contract between leaders and subordinates, loyalty is the primary service that is exchanged for the leader's coverage—unquestioning, blind loyalty. Once someone has come under the coverage of a certain leader, it is not considered appropriate for him to critique that leader's behavior. Any person who does critique the leader assumes the posture of a challenger.

If accountability for leadership cannot come from community laws or from the constituency, then, we may ask, where does it come from? In the African context, accountability comes from above, from a higher personal authority. Even if a leader himself does not have a superior, like a governing board, his parents, ancestors, and clan elders would still be perceived as having some degree of authority to call him to account, at least at a personal level, for his behavior.

A leader's peers can also be a source of accountability. As his equals, they have the right to ask questions and offer feedback in a way that subordinates do not. A peer's freedom to be candid can go a long way in promoting reasonable thinking from a leader.

For example, in the traditional family arrangement, a husband is head of the household and is not accountable to his wife or to household rules for his behavior. If a wife has a problem with him that he chooses not to take seriously, she will often appeal for help to his superiors (parents, uncles, grandfather) or to his peers (brothers, cousins), with the expectation that they will be able to reason with him on her behalf.

Presidential exceptions

I was in Africa in 1997–1998, when American President Bill Clinton was being tried in court for lying under oath. What caught the attention of my African friends was that President Clinton had to stand trial, like a common civilian. And then, to the astonishment of my friends, he was actually impeached! The American justice system proved to be more powerful than the president himself.

Some African presidents have faced serious charges of crimes against humanity at the International Court of Human Rights, but no African president has been ousted by a court of law in his own country. My African friends found it baffling that the president of the United States himself did not have some way to get exemption from U.S. Federal law.

Juma: Leadership is for life.

Wesley: A role of leadership is usually time-limited.

Respect for age is one of the cardinal values of the African worldview.[4] As a leader advances through years, his credibility and influence continually increase. There is no concept of resignation; the status he accrues is his to keep until his death.

Perhaps we could compare it to the way we think of heroes. Unlike a position like "chairman" or "CEO," a hero does not retire when he reaches 65 or comes to the end of a term. He does not step down or pass on his duties to someone else. A hero never retires; he never loses rank; and neither do African leaders.

If a younger man is given authority over a certain area, he is still obligated to show deference to the older men around him as his elders, as his seniors. In the African setup, there is no time when a younger person legitimately overrides or supersedes his elders. Like parenting, leadership is for life.

Conclusion

The hierarchy in African communities is believed to be ordained by God as a conduit of order and harmony. Although leaders are hierarchically distant, Africa's communal lifestyle holds all the members of a community closely together. The "biggest" members and the "smallest" members are tied to one another through an assumed level of genuine compassion. Their distance is held in check by their warm, personal connection to the people they lead.

The litmus test for any leader is how well he has provided for his "children." As the Ugandan proverb says, "Show your superiority by providing for others."

---

[4] See Adeyemo (2009:16) for more on the "Cardinal Values of the African Worldview."

Questions for reflection

1. What did you learn about cultural relevance from this chapter or think about for the first time?
2. Which of the African perspectives presented seemed the most different to you from your way of thinking?
3. When have you observed African friends' behaviors that connected with the observations in this chapter?
4. As a Westerner, what cultural mistakes do you think you may be most likely to make?
5. What ideas from this chapter would you like to discuss further with an African friend?

Recommended reading on leadership

Leading with Cultural Intelligence, by David Livermore (2010). Instead of focusing on the nuances of one specific culture, this book looks at the core of culturally competent leadership, which is applicable in any context. Livermore presents a four-step model for becoming an adept leader anywhere around the world. With current research, case studies, and statistics, this book will help you develop and leverage your cultural competence. It is an ideal step deeper into the material from this chapter.

8

Labor, Loyalty, and Lounging Around: Navigating Concepts of Work

You are beautiful, but learn to work; you cannot eat your beauty.
(African proverb)

In 1978, American President Jimmy Carter facilitated critical meetings between two other world leaders—Egypt's President Anwar El Sadat and Israel's Prime Minister Menachem Begin. Their epic task was to chart a solution for the unraveling conflict in the Middle East, which was expected, at the time, to imminently erupt into a full-scale war.

With so much at stake, the three men went into twelve days of secret negotiations. At the end of the first day, the world waited expectantly for news. But there was none. The second day passed, and still no news.

It turns out that the men took the first two days—more than 10 percent of their total time together—to get to know each other on a personal level. They were chatting over coffee and learning the names of each other's grandchildren. The Camp David Accords were the result of their subsequent work.

Employment

Relationship versus task orientation

In the work setting, a basic difference between cultures is whether we emphasize relationships or tasks. Although work contexts in Africa vary with factors like urbanization and proximity to Western business models, Africans tend to be relationship-oriented, and Westerners tend to be task oriented in the work place.

President Carter, a Westerner, changed history through effective work with his colleagues from relationship-oriented cultures. He gives us a lovely model of what can happen when we prioritize task and relationship together.

The chart below notes some common differences between a task-focused and a relationship-focused work setting. Expatriates who develop fluency in the African concept of work are more likely to be comfortable, respected, and effective.

Table 8.1. Task focus versus relationship focus

Task	Relationship
tendency to move straight to business—relationships come later	tendency to establish comfortable relationships and a sense of mutual trust before getting down to business
keep most relationships with co-workers impersonal	have personal relationships with co-workers
sacrifice leisure time and time with family in favor of work	sacrifice work in favor of leisure time and time with family
define people based on what they do	define people based on who they are
get to know co-workers and colleagues quickly but usually superficially	get to know co-workers and colleagues slowly and in depth
use largely impersonal selection criteria in hiring (such as résumés or test scores)	use largely personal selection criteria (such as family connections) when hiring
allow work to overlap with personal time	do not allow work to impinge on personal life

From Peterson 2004:52. Used with permission.

Paying jobs are prized as a source of economic stability as well as social status, but paid employment is not available for many people in the African context. Consider that in 2013 the unemployment rate in Botswana was 18 percent, in South Africa it was 24 percent, and in Mauritania it was 31 percent. (By comparison, the unemployment rate that same year was 7 percent in Canada and 5 percent in Germany.)

Juma: Work is not available for much of our population.

Wesley: Work is available for most people who want it.

In spite of extremely high unemployment rates, African people employ a variety of strategies that stretch and share resources, such that large populations are able to stay alive, albeit at a basic economic level. These strategies may look strange to us because we rely on different strategies.

For example, you may notice employees in African businesses standing around idly, especially during low business hours. We might interpret this as "inefficiency" in staffing, but in Africa there seems to be a preference to employ more than the absolute minimum number of people, or even to tolerate low-performing employees, rather than squeeze absolute efficiency out of a small cadre of employees.

Over-staffing is one way to mitigate some of the impact of high unemployment. Although employees are usually paid low wages, more people have some amount of income, and the community is better able to survive.

Juma: The line between work and personal time is ambiguous.

Wesley: There is usually a definitive line between work and personal time.

Many Westerners believe there is an invisible, but firm, line around work space (or working hours). Work is a time for focus and efficiency, aimed at the needs of the employer. When at work, it may be embarrassing to be caught doing personal tasks, like checking Facebook, because work time is understood to be separate from personal time.

African people tend to make less of a distinction between work time and personal time. A person works, yes, but does not suspend his relationships just because he is at work. He continues to be a friend, neighbor, or parent.

Like any other African setting, the work setting is a relational space; it is common to find people leisurely chatting, sending and receiving text messages, and so on, without a sense that the work hours are so distinctly different from the rest of life. "Our society is completely social—and so is our work," says an African friend named Nafula.

This behavior does not necessarily mean what we might interpret it to mean in our home contexts; it only means that African culture defines the perimeters around work in its own way.

> **Juma: We are more concerned about having good relationships than about working efficiently.**
>
> **Wesley: We are more concerned about working efficiently than about having good relationships.**

Westerners may be friendly and warm, says Lanier (2000:27), "but when needing to get a job done or answer a question factually, he or she is completely focused on the task at hand." From my American standpoint, I see good working relationships as a bonus, in that I would rather have good relationships than bad, but I am more concerned about satisfactory work than about satisfactory relationships in my work place.

In Africa, harmonious and balanced relationships are more important than getting work done efficiently. Although it is stressful when tasks are not completed in good time, if we are forced to choose between efficiency and harmony, it is seen as appropriate to prioritize human relationships.

For example, African colleagues usually take time to greet each other and perhaps catch up after the weekend, before sitting down at their desks. It's important for Africans to have a feeling of positive connection with their colleagues before they launch into work. We might say that harmonious relationships are a prerequisite for effective work.

"Wasting" time in chit-chat

An African proverb says, "If you want to walk fast, walk alone; if you want to walk far, walk together." This saying acknowledges that, indeed, working with others usually slows things down, but long-term effectiveness depends on relationships. Good work and good relationships are inseparable. It's never a waste of time to cultivate smooth relationships at work. Harmony, not efficiency, is the highest value.[1]

---

[1] An African interviewee articulated this difference, and recommended it as part of cross-cultural competency for Westerners.

Lost lab reports

A nurse at the American Embassy in Nairobi told me this story:

"I hired an assistant for my secretary. Soon after, my secretary mentioned some concerns about the woman's work—most significantly, documents and lab reports were ending up in the wrong files. "Let's deal with this right away," I said. "This is a medical office, and files simply must be managed properly. I'm going to give her a warning."

But my secretary begged me not to. "Give her time!" she insisted. "She is new and just needs more time to adapt to the job."

Two weeks later, when I realized that files were still being mismanaged, I went to my new assistant. "This is not working," I said. "Thanks for helping us out for these weeks, but tomorrow will be your last day."

The minute my secretary heard what had happened, she came flying into my office, appalled. "How could you do this?" she demanded. "You can't just fire her."

"You asked me to give her time, and I did. She's had three weeks, and she hasn't made any improvements. What else was I supposed to do?"

"We could have found ways to make it work," my secretary insisted.

Before long, the assistant started working for a different department in the Embassy. My secretary was upset: "What am I supposed to say to her when I bump into her? This has totally ruined our relationship."

"If you see her," I said, "you just say hello. It's no big deal."

But it was a huge deal for her. In fact, the incident created a lot of tension between my secretary and me for a while."

Relationally-Informed Time Management

When Westerners go to a meeting, we are often very aware of the time. As the clock begins to slide past the official start time, our African colleagues leisurely converse with each other, but we become increasingly tense.

We might even be tempted to say something like, "Let's stop wasting time and get to work." This would be a rather crass comment in the African world, to insinuate that time spent on friendships is wasteful.

I recommend that, in Africa, we take our cues from our African colleagues. If they spend the first hour of an official meeting chatting informally, let's make sure we're in the middle of the crowd. People will eventually settle down to business, and the meeting will probably flow better once participants are feeling good about each other.

I recommend that Westerners prioritize building and maintaining relationships with African colleagues more than we normally would in our home context. Specifically, we can learn the protocols used for maintaining professional relationships, including the use of polite language, proper introductions, acknowledging others, and maintaining good relations. We can make it easier on ourselves by planning extra time to nurture these relationships.

Juma: Start business with relationship.
Wesley: Start business with business.

A well-mannered person in Africa always starts a conversation—even a business conversation—with friendly dialogue. Greetings and small talk create an important feel-good atmosphere between people. "Before attempting to do business with an African," says Maranz, "it is essential to establish at least a minimal personal basis for carrying on the transaction" (2001:172). The African way says *"Let's be friends first, and then we'll sort out the details."*

The African approach makes sense in that context where there is no formal system for contract enforcement or quality control. For example, there's no way to put a lien on a property, or file a formal complaint. Instead, Africans are more likely to appeal to an on-going relationship as the basis for quality services.

Since relational equity brings stability to business relationships, Africans prefer to work with people who are, to some extent, their friends. Besides, friendship usually guarantees better service. In communal cultures, "treating one's friends better than others is natural and ethical and is a sound business practice" say Hofstede, Hofstede, and Minkov (2010:121).

No straight answers, no safari

A friend from California tells this story of a time when he misjudged the importance of friendship in African business dealing:

"I wanted to take my wife on a game drive, so I went to the place where safari company drivers park their vans during the days while waiting for business. I approached one driver and asked, "How much do you charge for a three-day safari?"

He grabbed my hand and began shaking it. "Come inside, and we will talk."

But I didn't want to get cornered in his office, with soda and a long conversation. I just wanted to find the guy with the lowest price, negotiate with him, and get it done.

"No," I insisted, "I just want to know how much you charge."

"Well that depends," he replied with a broad smile, now putting his arm across my shoulders. "You are my friend. Come inside, friend; we can do business."

"I just want a straight answer," I said, irritated now. I shook his arm off my shoulder and walked away.

> **Juma: A critique of someone's idea (or performance) is a critique of him or her personally.**
>
> **Wesley: We can criticize someone's idea without attacking him or her as a person.**

Western people treat a person as being somewhat separate, or removed, from her ideas. If a Western friend asks what you think about, say, a decision he made or a project he's proposing, you can openly mention points where you disagree with him, and as long as you are nice about it, he probably won't be insulted.

Since we talk to each other this way, we might assume that the rest of the world does too. Quite the contrary, among many cultures, including the African context, a person is not seen as being differentiated from his ideas, his performance, or his actions. He is one person; all these things are together. To criticize someone's ideas or behavior is to criticize him personally, and in spite of tact and our best intentions, it will probably be taken as a personal insult.

For example, I have noticed that it is common for Western visitors, fresh off the plane, to verbalize negative critiques about Africa. "How can people drive in this mess?" Or "Why don't they just…." We don't mean to insult our local hosts (in our minds, a person is also separate from his national group), but our complaints can come across the wrong way to our hosts.

Compared to how we might interact with Western colleagues, we can try to be more circumspect and diplomatic with African colleagues. It never works in our favor to be perceived as overly critical. Chapter 6 on communication and conflict discusses some considerations for the polite management of delicate issues.

Evaluating the Workplace

Underneath the modern Western concept of work is the industrial view of workers as units of production. When a "unit" flounders in his production, his usefulness to the employer decreases, which in turn may jeopardize his job.

> **Juma: We allow space for the humanity of others, including employees.**
>
> **Wesley: We sometimes think of employees as functional units of production.**

I have observed that Africans tend to accept people's humanness in the workplace more than do Westerners. For example, people will need time to care for sick children, entertain out-of-town visitors, and attend to social obligations. Such interference with work should not be penalized; it is part of what it means to be human and to participate in the human community.

Juma: Hiring and firing are relational issues.

Wesley: Hiring and firing are performance issues.

When a colleague is dealing with a difficult situation at home, there is an understanding that this person should be handled with extra care in the work place. "Vulnerability obligates others at work to be gentle with you," says Nakesa. When someone is having a hard time, "other people should postpone difficult conversations, and so on."

This humanity allowance is often included in institutional policies. For example, employers are often expected to give an employee several days off, with full pay, when he needs to go to his rural community for a relative's funeral. Employers may also be expected to provide advances of salary for certain holidays or family situations such as a newborn's naming ceremony (Maranz 2001:176). Likewise, if there is a quota for sick days, African employers may opt not to enforce it; it would be dehumanizing to treat a person like a machine (as though anyone can control how often he gets sick).

Western leaders can be aware that they may need to bend and flex with their African staff more than they are accustomed to. Sometimes people take advantage of this gentle personnel policy, but not all requests for leniency are exploitative. Whatever boundaries you do settle on, it is important that African staff know they are honored as human beings, regardless of their productive output for a given day.

Solidarity in the Workplace

For Africans who are in positions to hire or lay off employees, there are social factors to consider as well as factors of performance.

Because of the spiritual value placed on smooth relationships, Africans may be reticent to fire underperforming employees. It's nearly impossible to fire someone without injuring the connection to them, and connections are seen as being more significant, more eternal, than job performance.

African employers are also aware of social factors when hiring new staff. Giving a position to a particular person is one way of honoring a friendship or ethnic connection. "In a collectivist culture," say Hofstede, Hofstede, and Minkov (2010:117), "an employer never hires just an individual, but rather a person who belongs to an in-group. The hiring process...always takes the in-group into account." Although performance is important, it is not the "bottom line."

"I can't fire her"

Nekesa is a Kenyan journalist I met at the party of a mutual friend. She is a member of the Luhya community, and shared this story with me from her own life:

"I had a house helper working for me, but she did a lousy job. She wasn't a good cook, and she was slow with the housework. But I could not bring myself to fire her. I knew I would run into her and her family members out in the community. So I told my husband, 'Since we can't fire her, let's just pray that she resigns.'

After ten years, she finally did! It was stressful at the time, but when we meet in public now, it's not awkward between us. I think we Africans have an attitude of 'doing whatever it takes' to preserve a relationship."

Juma: Loyalty is usually highest to a certain in-group.

Wesley: In the work place, loyalty is to company interests.

The highest loyalty of an African person usually lies with a particular in-group, typically an ethnic group, of which he is a member. We can expect that he will act according to the interest of that group (which may not always coincide with his individual interest) above other, more temporary affiliations he may have, including his place of employment. Ethnic and other in-group differences play an important role in workplace functions, and it is extremely important for managers to be attentive to these factors.

One of the implications of this reality is that workplace decisions may be based on many factors other than what is best for the company. For example,

- Contracts may be given to relatives and friends because they are members of the in-group, rather than because they provide the best service at the best price.
- Positions may be given on the basis of family ties rather than merit (qualification).

- Poor performance may be overlooked when the employee is an in-group member.
- In-group members may receive better services or better prices than non-members.

So long as it is an impersonal entity that stands to lose out, such as the government or a large corporation, there is a sense that it is legitimate to misuse it for the sake of bettering one's group. Practices that are defined in law as "fraud" or "embezzlement" may be largely ignored as long as the target is not one's personal friends and relatives. Westerners may interpret this as taking advantage of the company, but Africans think of it as loyalty to their family. It's one way to share resources.

According to one African saying, "If one man becomes wealthy, his village does not benefit, but if the village becomes wealthy, everyone benefits." When a company turns a profit, then, it seems appropriate for the whole community to benefit rather than only a few people at the top. Why should only one man (or several) benefit? Through kickbacks, in-group hiring, and other informal perks, the profits of the company benefit the whole village.

I am not suggesting that Westerners in Africa should capitulate to this way of managing loyalties, but simply making the observation that in-group alliances play a significant hand in the African workplace, albeit often unseen (to us), and we can work smarter when we're aware of it.

Relational Networking

Because business in Africa is seen to flow congruently with personal relationships, the interplay between business and personal concerns can, at times, become rather convoluted.

People commonly patronize the businesses of their friends. This economic boost is assumed to be part of friendship. That is to say, purchases are often made on the basis of relationship more than on the basis of the product.

Therefore, when it comes to business, it's important to make friends with many potential clients.

> **Juma: It is normal, or at least acceptable, for personal and business concerns to overlap.**
>
> **Wesley: Mixing personal and business concerns is a conflict of interest.**

One way people develop these relationships is through benefits, or "kickbacks," which are gifts given to customers. However, it is common for kickbacks to go to the individual who makes a purchase on behalf of his company, rather than to the company itself.

In the West, we also use incentives for sales. However, there is a feeling that the incentives should be known up front. A person who is biased, due to personal kickbacks and under-the-table commissions, might be seen as unethical, or as compromised by a "conflict of interest."

Kickbacks (and other "alignments" of interests) are not necessarily seen as violations of some ethical code in Africa. This system rises out of an environment where personal, professional, and economic interests are assumed to run together. If you get into a situation where it feels like the alignment of interests is becoming unethical, I recommend that you discuss it carefully with a trusted, mature African friend before making a decision on how you will respond.

An American needs a house

An American friend tells this story:

"When I moved to Nairobi, I was told that a certain local staff member at my organization was responsible to help incoming employees find apartments. After she had set up several appointments for me with one realtor, I asked to see some apartments from another realtor, hoping to make the realtors compete against each other to give me the best price. She was reluctant to do so, but eventually agreed to show me an apartment that was listed with someone else.

I really liked that apartment. But when I told my colleague that I wanted to rent it, she refused. She said, "Actually, we've already signed a contract for you on the first apartment."

I was angry at her overt attempt to manipulate me. I assumed that she had some sort of insider deal with the first realtor—maybe he was a relative and/or was giving her kickbacks. Whatever it was about, it was very clear that my interests were not her top priority. I reported the incident to Human Resources, but nothing ever came of it."

Juma: Work agreements and targets are often ambiguous.

Wesley: Work agreements are usually explicit and put in writing.

In contrast to the Western model, where work agreements are usually explicit and formalized through official documentation, African job descriptions, project plans, and contracts may not be written down at all, or—if written—be largely ignored.

Perhaps there's less perceived need for documentation because most African people share a tacit understanding of the "Big Man" system (sometimes referred to as the patron-client system). As we discussed in the chapter on Leadership, the African "Big Man" system has a specific way of organizing work expectations, not through any type of formal documentation, but through the social dynamic between people.

When Westerners are partnering with Africans, sometimes we prefer to use documentation, which helps us feel that expectations are explicit and somehow more binding. While these are legitimate concerns, we can bear in mind that African people may have their own concept of what the documentation means.

Charles, from South Sudan, having worked with both African- and Western-run organizations, explains it this way: When a written contract is used, "it is understood as a statement about our relationship, right now, not as a statement of deliverables, time, and roles."

Moreover, African targets tend to be more people-oriented and abstract (such as "influence" or "growth"), rather than defined in terms of numbers and time. As long as it's helping the community, Charles comments, "a project that gets finished ten years later than expected, over budget, and looking nothing like the original blue print would still be considered a success."

He suggests that Westerners might be more satisfied with African partners if we would think of official documents as statements of intent, or starting points. The goal itself may be something of a moving target, so stay engaged.

Let me add a reminder about the importance of cultivating relationships throughout the life of a project. Although official documents may be largely ignored, positive relationships can do wonders to hold together a deal.

Juma: We make decisions in a circular way.

Wesley: We make decisions in a linear way.

When a decision needs to be made in a meeting of Westerners, we usually follow a linear procedure, something like the following figure.

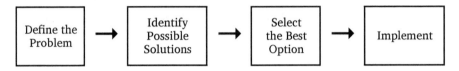

Figure 8.1. Linear decision making.

In a meeting of Africans, the process is usually more circular, as illustrated by the following figure:

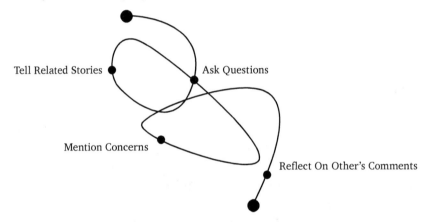

Figure 8.2. Circular decision making.

The objective of the African decision-making style is to find a lasting solution that is acceptable to everyone (regardless of how long it takes). Everyone has a chance to voice his perspective, and the group processes information together. Eventually, one course of action usually emerges as the most meritorious, and the decision is considered "made."

The African path to decision can be slow, yet dizzying for Westerners. Especially when time constraints begin to tighten, we may feel frustrated by the round-and-round nature of the discussion, and even tempted to seize control of the meeting. Our expectation of efficiency can quickly be interpreted as aggression, impatience, and tactlessness, all of which sabotage our work. Instead, we can honor our colleagues by pacing with their model, which has worked for them for thousands of years.

Juma: We prefer to cooperate with and contribute to the group.

Wesley: We prefer to perform individually.

In societies that are more individual-oriented (rather than collective-oriented), workers generally perform best when working on their own. Hofstede, Hofstede, and Minkov cite one study in which American managers were found to perform their highest when operating individually, with their names on items they produced, and they performed their worst when operating as a group and anonymously (2010:121).

Although it's easy to assume that others function like us, this is not the case. We may find that African colleagues, like most people in collective cultures, do their best work when functioning as a team. Working in a group, they can contribute toward a shared goal without being conspicuous individually. Group bonuses and incentives might be more effective than individual rewards.

Given the general preference to fit in, a person's individual performance appraisals can be exceedingly embarrassing as an open discussion where one's flaws are laid bare. If possible, it is better to use other forms of feedback in which people can maintain their sense of dignity.

Juma: We might not speak up, even if we disagree.

Westley: We are usually candid with our suggestions and critiques.

When African colleagues are quiet in a meeting, we may take their silence to mean that they basically agree with what is being decided and don't have any further suggestions or critiques to add. We know, at least, that we can usually count on Western colleagues to speak their minds; so can't we assume the same of Africans?

In the African setting, however, silence doesn't necessarily equal agreement. In some situations, it is considered tactful to remain silent, even when you do have something important you'd like to say.

For example, if everyone in a work group is moving toward a certain decision, an individual may prefer not to mention his concerns because it would be embarrassing to single oneself out for having a different opinion. "We don't want to be seen giving an opinion differing from others in the group," confirms Nekesa. "We may not speak up [in a group setting], even if opinions are invited." In this case, silence can be a statement of solidarity with the group; no one wants to be seen as a dissenter.

A younger adult may also be hesitant to voice opinions in the presence of a higher-status adult. "When people of higher status are in the room," says Nafula, "we withhold our opinions. The leader must invite opinions. Even then, we may not speak up." In this case, silence can be a statement of respect for the other person.

If the higher-status person is the one pushing for a certain course of action, group members may be even more unlikely to be open about their thoughts. It is considered very inappropriate to contradict or critique the idea of a high-status person. If someone were to do so, it would likely be interpreted as a public power challenge.

Compared to Westerners, Africans may be more hesitant to express their opinions and ideas, especially depending on the tone of the group and people who are present. Candid feedback is more likely to be shared in the context of a private conversation.

Juma: If something is working right now, it's working.

Wesley: We want things to work long-term.

Africans seem to be more content than Westerners with solutions that work right now; if something works today, it's working, and that's good enough.

Maranz refers to this as the African "spirit of just getting by." He observes that "People tend to accept immediate, cheap, or even quasi-legal solutions when dealing with business matters, rather than take care of matters properly—especially if it requires spending more money or time" (2001:182).

A friend of mine who sells cars in Nairobi, Kenya, reports that, in his experience, Africans prefer to purchase cars owned by foreigners. "People prefer to buy cars from expatriates because of the stereotype that they take much better care of their vehicles" (regular oil changes, long-term maintenance, etc.), he says. Although changing the oil is not complicated or expensive, Africans generally prefer to fix things after they break, rather than give "undue" attention to something that is operating perfectly well right now.

We can expect that African colleagues may feel less urgency to solve problems that, technically, do not yet exist. The best time to fix something is right after it breaks down.

Juma: We are willing to "let the fool pay."

Wesley: We like people to be up front about pertinent information.

Africans may be less likely than Westerners to be up front with information that is important to know in the work setting. There are several explanations for this.

This is partly a byproduct of living in the present; when plans have not yet been made, it is impossible to give information in advance. It's also connected to concepts of privacy; people are not as likely to offer their personal ideas or things they know, especially when there is a status difference. Africans may prefer to wait to be asked. There are times when one stands to benefit by refraining from offering information, and if confronted, he can truthfully state that "I was not asked."

It is the duty of the person initiating a project to collect relevant data. It is not the duty of the recipient to offer it. Nakesa introduced me to the expression, *"Let the fool pay,"* or in other words, if a person initiating business fails to practice due diligence, it's his own problem. There is little incentive to offer information, especially information that—if shared—could compromise a potential benefit to the person who is holding it.

"Let the fool pay"

A short-term American team went to visit a Kenyan church of their denomination. The church was located in a slum area of Nairobi, with about forty members, and the building was made of sheets of corrugated tin.

The Americans were shocked by the poverty, the lack of hygiene, and the many hungry children they observed around the church. So, at the end of their trip, the group decided to donate any money they had left over from the trip. "How can we bless your church?" they asked the pastor.

"Well," replied the pastor, "the youth want to do outreaches in the community, but they cannot because they don't have an electric keyboard and sound system." So the visitors purchased an electric keyboard and a sound system for the church.

The church members were thrilled with the enormous gift, and the Americans were pleased that they had been able to help out. But they failed to ask some relevant questions. Does the church building have electricity?

Are there any youth in the first place? Does anyone know how to use a keyboard? The Americans didn't ask, and the church members were shrewd enough not to bring it up.

Conclusion

Working in our home environment is hard enough; the office politics, competition, and conflicts we deal with at home potentially become much more complex and slippery on the international scene. But we haven't left it to luck. We are learning to work with African colleagues in ways that are suitable for everyone.

Oddly enough, sometimes it's slowing down that opens the door for real work to happen. If we try to force a quick business deal with people from relationship-oriented cultures, according to Hofstede, Hofstede, and Minkov (2010:121), we push ourselves further away from the "friend" category and more and more into the "non-friend" category, which ultimately leads to less cooperation.

Jimmy Carter worked for peace in the Middle East by drinking coffee. It's an important lesson for all of us. Fill up your mug, and keep smiling.

Questions for reflection

1. What did you learn from this chapter or think about for the first time?
2. Which of the African perspectives presented seemed the most different to you from your way of thinking?
3. When have you observed African friends' behaviors that connected with the observations in this chapter?
4. As a Westerner, what cultural mistakes do you think you may be most likely to make?
5. What ideas from this chapter would you like to discuss further with an African friend?

Recommended reading on cross-cultural work

So You're Going Overseas: A Handbook for Personal and Professional Success, by Stewart Black and Hal Gregersen (1998). This book is a pre-departure guide to moving abroad with your job. One chapter discusses cultural competence, and the others cover logistics, such as financial implications, adjustments, and considerations for the family.

The Cultural Intelligence Difference: Master the one Skill You Can't Do Without in Today's Global Economy, by David Livermore (2011). Livermore is a thought leader in the area of cultural intelligence. This book gives insight into leadership and thriving in a culturally diverse workplace. Each copy of the book gives access to an academically valid CQ assessment online.

African Friends and Money Matters by David Maranz (2001) has an excellent chapter on business transactions, which expands on what is said here.

Cross-Cultural Connections: Stepping out and Fitting In Around the World by Duane Elmer (2002) has a section on "cultural differences that confuse," in which Elmer discusses the dynamic between task and relationship and several other factors of great relevance in the work place.

Epilogue

We have covered a lot of ground in this book, learning about African culture and quite possibly reflecting in new ways on our own cultural background. In conclusion, I want to share five tips to keep us sharp: They are as applicable for old-timers in Africa as they are for people whose clothes are not yet faded.

1. *Keep learning about the African country where you live (or are visiting).*

I was seventeen when I came to Africa for the first time, and admit with chagrin that I made no attempt whatsoever to learn about the continent before I arrived. I was a busy person back then. It wasn't immediately clear to my teenage mind how information would help me with the things that were truly important. (I already had packed my hair spray, the main thing of true importance.) It was a miserable trip. There were no catastrophes per se, but I was completely unprepared for the rigors of the adjustment process.

The information we take in—through reading, watching educational clips, talking with Africans in our home countries or Westerners who work in Africa—educates us and forms our expectations. Well informed, realistic expectations are one of the simplest ways to make things easy for yourself.

Part of my problem on that first Africa trip was that I didn't know what to learn about. In the appendix section of this book, I have included a simple chart as a starting point. I use this chart in cultural competency trainings

147

to help incoming Westerners learn about their African host country *vis a vis* their passport country. As more specific interests emerge, our own curiosity will pull us forward into higher-level research.

2. *Brace yourself for stress as you develop cultural competency.*

We tend to underestimate how quickly and utterly a new environment can drain our energy. Checking into a hotel room in Dar es Salaam one weekend, I found myself darkly irritable. I wasn't hungry, tired, or overly uncomfortable from the muggy air. It was just my first time in Dar, and I hate that feeling of being lost. How will I get drinking water? Will I be able to sleep with the street noise? Managing even the most basic human needs takes extra energy in new situations, and that extra energy, then, is not available to be used for other things. If we let ourselves consider that new experiences require new levels of energy, we can brace ourselves adequately.

In the appendix section, I have included a brief chart that describes three stages of cultural adaptation—from being at home, to the transition period, to establishing a new home. I use this chart with people to help them sort out how they are feeling. The goal is to slowly make movement toward the right hand side of the chart, toward adjustment to the new environment.

3. *Intentionally develop your social circles.*

As much as we need friends at home, we need support even more when we're in new situations. Be proactive. With a few rare exceptions, I have never been freely offered a friendship or network, much like we've never been handed a free salary. These are things we work for. Who do you want to get to know? How can you do it? Don't wait for someone else to take the initiative—you are the rightful owner of your own social circles.

After reading *Never Eat Alone: And Other Secrets to Success, One Relationship at a Time,* (Ferrazzi, 2005) I've made a weekly practice of initiating a coffee date with a friend (or an acquaintance that I hope will become a friend). I call it a "practice" because it takes discipline to keep reaching out to people I don't know well, from a variety of social circles, especially on weeks when my Google calendar is hectic. Nevertheless, this habit has resulted in a wide range of contacts with both local people and other expatriates.

Interaction with local players lends itself to fluency in the local scene. A broad network ensures that you will know who to call when there's a problem, and when the time comes that your closest friends all finish their contracts and move home, you will have other budding friendships to fall back on.

4. *Consider how to build your linguistic competence.*

> Roughly speaking, most [expatriates] know about as much of the culture as they do of the language—at least no more. So if you can just "get by" in the local language, you probably cannot do more than just "get by" in the local culture. (Stafford 1986:90)

What would it take for you to take the next step into the local language? Missionary author Tim Stafford observed that expatriates' cultural competence often matches their level of linguistic competence—an observation that sobered me and resulted in my scheduling more lessons with my language teacher.

We can always think of reasons not to study language: it's hard, it's embarrassing to fumble our words, and it takes a lot of time. These reasons will never go away. The advantages of linguistic competence will never go away either: increased likelihood of genuine friendships, the ability to navigate local situations on our own, and general comfort in our host country. We get to choose.

In situations where it is impossible to develop local language fluency, I recommend that we focus our energy on speaking our own language in a culturally competent way. Here are some suggestions from Peterson [adapted with permission] (2004:190-195).

Avoid idiomatic expressions. For example, instead of using phrases like "the sky is the limit," we can say what we mean in plain English: "This has a lot of potential."

Use body language to your best advantage. For example, in asking for the bill at a restaurant, one might pair the request with the hand motion of writing a bill.

Speak slowly and clearly (but not loudly). Between native speakers of our own language, we may slur our words together, "I shdnna done tha'." With non-native English speakers we can do everyone a favor and articulate our words with clarity.

If the listener seems confused, offer examples. Do you get a blank stare when you ask the cashier "Do you take credit cards?" Try giving her options: "Visa? Master Card?"

Learn the "six basics" of the local language, which are, according to Brooks Peterson (2004:199), the bare minimum of courtesy to our hosts: "Yes," "no," "please," "thank you," "hello," and "good bye."

Notice nonverbal behavior. Do your African friends shake hands, embrace, or kiss upon meeting? Are greetings between women different from greetings between men? How do people greet each other when their hands are full or dirty (being caught in the middle of a task)? Awareness of nonverbal encoding helps us send the messages about ourselves that we mean to send.

5. *Take your cultural competence back home with you.*

We travelers have great potential to irritate the people at home by talking incessantly about Africa or otherwise failing to enter into our friends' reality. In the same way that we stretch ourselves to graciously accept the local African culture, we can also be gracious with the people in our passport country who stayed home. They cannot identify with the things we've experienced; people can only identify with experiences they have had themselves. Again, it's our job to bridge the gap.

Although no one else can fully identify with *all* of our experiences, there are many shared experiences that can connect us to the people at home. I enjoy talking with old friends about our children, our hobbies, our gardens, and pets. There are updates to swap about people we both know. The exercise of learning to build friendships with Africans, whose culture and language are so different from mine, has taught me, ironically, how to relate more meaningfully with old friends from back home whose life experiences are very different from mine.

The goal of cross-cultural competence is genuine connection between dissimilar people. Without capering off into endless evaluation of how good or bad, exotic or bland, another culture is, we hone our focus on acquiring the skills and attitudes we need in order to behave in ways that are acceptable and meaningful to the local people. Cultural competence is all about making adjustments to our personal style for the purpose of living as a well-adjusted adult in a new environment.

Culturally Competent Westerners

- Are able to conduct daily living without experiencing excessive strain from the local people's habits.
- Understand what our local friends communicate, even when their communication is indirect.
- Work effectively.
- Are not exasperated by "normal" African organization and scheduling.
- Are perceived as trustworthy.
- Maintain the dignity of all involved parties in the midst of conflict management.
- Avoid unintentionally insulting others.
- Can be generous without going broke.
- Avoid inadvertently making promises that they can't keep.
- Can host and be hosted comfortably by local people.

In the first pages of this book, I told a story about a British man in Nigeria, who, as a "proper" gentleman, opened doors for Nigerian ladies as a gesture of courtesy. Now that he is aware of his faux pas, I hope that, if he is still in Nigeria today, he can be found bravely leading the way through doorways, promptly disposing of any reptiles, and enamoring the ladies of Nigeria.

Appendix A:
Cultural Adjustment Process

Cultural Adjustment Process

At HOME, we...	In TRANSITION, we experience...	With ADJUSTMENT, we...
• Understand the environment	• Disorientation	• Are able to build meaningful relationships with local people
• Know who we are (have a sense of identity)	• Changes in important relationships	• Are able to do our work without excessive frustration
• Know our roles in the family and community	• Changes in identity & self-image	• Establish new routines; this makes our environment become more predictable
• Have established routines	• The former mental map of reality is not adequate for new experiences	• Live without undue fear and anxiety
• Know how to operate competently in the environment and in the language	• Our expectations are confused	• Understand how this experience fits and contributes to our lives
• Have a mental map of reality and know where we're at on it	• Frustration, which can lead to depression, exhaustion, withdrawal	• Establish ways to effectively stay connected to people from home
• Are surrounded by people who know us	• Anxiety, and sometimes our old traumas resurface	• Are reasonably comfortable with local customs
• Are comfortable, and if something goes wrong, we know what to do to get comfortable again	• Difficulty in getting things done	• Have realistic expectations about others and ourselves
• Are familiar with ways to take care of ourselves	• Loneliness, distance from support	• Find new ways to take care of ourselves
	• Inefficiency	• Achieve familiarity: *"Although this place is different from home, I am successfully building a life here."*
	• Uncertainty with strange customs, unreliable electric, water, technology	
	• Inability to "read" symbols (behavioral, environmental, in communication)	
	• Frustration with the host culture, perhaps that *"This must be a bad place, because I feel bad being here."*	

"My life is normal" – – – → *"This place is crazy!"* – – – → *"There is more than one way to live normally"*

153

Appendix B: Data Points for Travelers

Place	My home country	My host country
Population		
Average income (per capita)		
Currency		
Language(s)		
Religion(s)		
Typical food		
Form of government		
First line of national anthem		
Four largest cities		
Literacy rate		
The top three income-producing industries in the national economy		
Major ethnic groups within the country		
Major illness/medical problems		
Significant wars in past 50 years		
What services are provided by the government free of charge?		
How are people from my country perceived?		

References

Adeyemo, Tokunboh. 2009. *Africa's enigma and leadership solutions.* Nairobi: Word Alive Publishers.

Black, J. Stewart, and Hal B. Gregersen. 1998. *So you're going overseas: A handbook for personal and professional success.* London: Global Business Publishers.

Corbett, Steve, and Brian Fikkert. 2009. *When helping hurts: Alleviating poverty without hurting the poor...or yourself.* Chicago: Moody Publishers.

Elmer, Duane. 1993. *Cross-cultural conflict: Building relationships for effective ministry.* Downers Grove, IL: InterVarsity Press.

Elmer, Duane. 2002. *Cross-cultural connections: Stepping out and fitting in around the world.* Downers Grove, IL: InterVarsity Press.

Ferrazzi, Keith. 2005. *Never eat alone: And other secrets to success, one relationship at a time.* Danvers, MA: Crown Business.

Goodenough, Ward H. 1971. *Culture, language and society.* Menlo Park, CA: Benjamin/Cummings.

Hiebert, Paul. 1986. *Anthropological insights for missionaries.* Seventeenth ed. Grand Rapids: Baker Books.

Hofstede, Geert. 2004-2017a. Cultural dimensions: Individualism. In ClearlyCultural.com. http://www.clearlycultural.com/geert-hofstede-cultural-dimensions/individualism/. Accessed October 9, 2017.

Hofstede, Geert. 2004-2017b. Cultural dimensions: Power-distance-index. In ClearlyCultural.com. http://www.clearlycultural.com/geert-hofstede-cultural-dimensions/power-distance-index. Accessed October 9, 2017.

Hofstede Geert, Gert Jan Hofstede, and Michael Minkov. 2010. *Cultures and organizations: Software of the mind*. Third Edition. New York: McGraw-Hill USA.

Jacobs, Donald R. 2012. *What a life! A memoir*. New York: Good Books.

Kirwen, Michael C. 1987/2008. *The missionary and the diviner: Contending theologies of Christian and African religions*. Maryknoll, NY: Orbis Books.

Kirwen, Michael C., ed. 2011. *African cultural knowledge: Themes and embedded beliefs*. Nairobi: MIAS Books.

Lanier, Sarah. 2000. *Foreign to familiar: A guide to understanding hot- and cold-climate cultures*. Hagerstown, MD: McDougal Publishing Company.

Lederleitner, Mary T. 2010. *Cross-cultural partnerships: Navigating the complexities of money and mission*. Downers Grove, IL: InterVarsity Press.

Livermore, David. 2006. *Serving with eyes wide open: Doing short-term missions with cultural intelligence*. Grand Rapids, MI: Baker Books.

Livermore, David. 2010. *Leading with cultural intelligence: The new secret to success*. New York: Amacom.

Livermore, David. 2011. *The cultural intelligence difference: Master the one skill you can't do without in today's global economy*. New York: Amacom. http://www.culturalq.com/docs/CQ-Difference-Chapter-1.pdf. Accessed October 9, 2017.

Magesa, Laurenti. 1997. *African religion: The moral traditions of abundant life*. Maryknoll, NY: Orbis Books.

Magesa, Laurenti. 2013a. Lecture at Tangaza College, Nairobi, November 2013.

Magesa, Laurenti. 2013b. *What is not sacred?: African spirituality*. Maryknoll, NY: Orbis Books.

Malunga, Chiku. 2009. *Understanding organizational leadership through ubuntu*. London: Adonis & Abbey Publishers.

Maranz, David. 2001. *African friends and money matters: Observations from Africa*. Publications in Ethnography 37. Dallas: SIL International and Museum of Cultures.

Mbiti, John S. 1969. *African religions and philosophy*. Gaborone: Heinemann Educational Botswana Ltd.

Mbiti, John S. 1989. *African religions and philosophy*. Second edition. Oxford: Heinemann Educational Publishers.

Mbiti, John S. 1991. *Introduction to African religion.* Second edition. Oxford: Heinemann Educational Publishers.

Mulder, Patty. 2013. Communication model by Albert Mehrabian. https://www.toolshero.com/communication-skills/communication-model-mehrabian/. Accessed October 9, 2017.

Muriu, Oscar. 2007. The African planter: Nairobi Chapel pastor on mission trips, and working well across cultures. An interview with Oscar Muriu. *Christianity Today International/Leadership Journal.* Spring 2007. Vol. XXVIII, No. 2.

Neufeld, Josiah. 2013. The way we give: Generosity can't always cross cultural and economic divides. *The Walrus.* December 2013, 41–44.

Peterson, Brooks. 2004. *Cultural intelligence: A guide to working with people from other cultures.* Yarmouth, ME: Intercultural Press, Inc.

Ramsey, Dave. 2003. *The total money makeover: A proven plan for financial fitness.* Nashville: Thomas Nelson, Inc.

Shaw, Perry. 2012. Patronage, exemption, and institutional policy. *Evangelical Missions Quarterly* 49(1):8–18.

Stafford, Tim. 1986. *The friendship gap: Reaching out across cultures.* Downers Grove, IL: Intervarsity Press.

Storti, Craig. 1999. *Figuring foreigners out: A practical guide.* Yarmouth, ME: Intercultural Press.

Storti, Craig. 2001. *The art of crossing cultures.* Second edition. London: Nicholas Brealey Publishing. Yarmouth, ME: Intercultural Press.

Whiteman, Darrell. 2015. Culture, values, and worldview: Anthropology for mission practice. Lecture presented at the Overseas Ministry Study Center, New Haven, CT, January 19–23, 2015.

Index

A

accountability 123
accounting 43, 44, 46. *See also* finance
adjustment 5, 8, 25, 147, 153
African perspective/philosophy xv, 30, 47, 63, 73, 105
ally/allies 50, 52, 62, 69, 70
ambiguity 14, 20
apology/apologize 23, 98, 99
asset(s) 42, 76, 117

B

banking 38
banks 69
bargaining 38, 41
belligerent 32
Big Man 139
blame 32, 97, 98
borrow/borrower/borrowing 31, 33, 36, 37, 41, 42. *See also* debt, lender, *and* loan
budget/budgeted 43, 139

C

ceremony 63, 73, 79, 106, 135
cluster 22
collectivist societies 58
communal(ist)/collective culture(s) 37, 133, 141. *See also* individualistic culture
communication 89–107
community 29, 30, 38, 56, 63, 74, 75, 80–86, 105, 112, 117, 118, 120, 124, 137
community gatherings 68
conflict 78, 86, 89, 91, 96, 99, 100, 105, 107
conflict of interest 138
credibility/credible 5, 116, 124
credit 35, 38
crisis/crises, crisis times 50, 51, 56, 62, 68, 78
(cross-)cultural competence v, 1, 2, 11, 29, 125, 149, 150
cross-cultural dialogue 90
culture clusters 9
culture(s) 2–11, 14, 28, 57, 110, 128, 135, 149
low-power/high-power distance

161

SIL International Publications
Additional Releases in the
Publications in Ethnography Series

44. The heart of the matter: Seeking the center in Maya-Mam language and culture, by Wesley M. Collins, 2015, 205 pp., ISBN 978-1-55671-375-0.
43. African friends and money matters. Second edition, by David E. Maranz, 2015, 293 pp., ISBN 978-1-55671-277-7.
42. Ensnared by AIDS: Cultural contexts of HIV and AIDS in Nepal, by David K. Beine, 2014, 357 pp., ISBN 978-1-55671-350-7.
41. The Norsk Høstfest: A celebration of ethnic food and ethnic identity, by Paul Thomas Emch, 2011, 121 pp., ISBN 978-1-55671-265-4.
40. Our company increases apace: History, language, and social identity in early colonial Andover, Massachusetts, by Elinor Abbot, 2007, 279 pp., ISBN 978-1-55671-169-5.
39. What place for hunters-gatherers in millenium three?, by Thomas N. Headland and Doris E. Blood, eds. 2002, 130 pp., ISBN 978-1-55671-132-9.
38. A tale of Pudicho's people, by Richard Montag, 2002, 181 pp., ISBN 978-1-55671-131-2.

SIL International Publications
7500 W. Camp Wisdom Road
Dallas, Texas 75236-5629 USA

General inquiry: publications_intl@sil.org
Pending order inquiry: sales@sil.org
www.sil.org/resources/publications

About the Author

Debbi DiGennaro moved from the United States to East Africa in 2008. Based in Nairobi with her family, she currently leads the regional team of a faith-based NGO.

DiGennaro holds a Master's Degree in Social Work from The Ohio State University. She leaned heavily on her background in the social sciences as she adjusted to the rhythms of work and relationships in Africa. In an effort to understand the new social reality, she interviewed, questioned, and read extensively, eventually getting involved in teaching sociology at African International University. DiGennaro regularly trains and coaches those experiencing new cultures. Her research, teaching, and friendship with Africans and expatriates eventually led to the writing of this book.

Visit her website at www.debbidigennaro.com.

CPSIA information can be obtained
at www.ICGtesting.com
Printed in the USA
BVHW040900180120
569929BV00010B/278

9 781556 713866